Mood Drinks is a seriously s...
collection of non-alcoholic
cocktails, created and
photographed by acclaimed
lifestyle photographer Gabriel
Cabrera. Gabriel has crafted
60 stylish recipes to help
reflect, enhance or shift your
mood. Each chapter groups
recipes by shared flavor profile,
carefully curated for that
particular mood. The result is an
array of delicious drinks made
with intentional and accessible
ingredients like fresh citrus,
seasonal fruits, super-steeped
teas, homemade bitters, and
salty brines.

...ks
...e,
like the Sleepy Cherries, made with tart
cherry, tangy orange peel and nutmeg,
or the Sesame Blanket, made with black
sesame, cinnamon and fennel seeds.

UPLIFT
Boost your energy with savory, spicy and
fizzy drinks that jolt your mood with a
nice bite of salt or spice. For a quick zing,
try the Shiso Cuke Sour, made with
cucumber, fresh shiso leaves and frosty
cocktail foam, or a Guava Brava, made with
guava nectar, plum vinegar and sumac.

CELEBRATE
Cheers with citrus, floral and fruit-forward
drinks full of personality and sparkle
like A Shot of Joy, made with jasmine tea,
cantaloupe and ginger, or the Fountain
of Beauty, made with elderflower and
non-alcoholic bubbly.

EXPLORE
Experiment with funky, fermented
and oddball drinks of edgy and curious
mixes like the Umamilada, made with
mushroom broth, tomato juice, pickle
brine and non-alcoholic beer, or the
Sage Away, made with cardamom and
green tea, or the Gochu Soda, made
with non-alcoholic aperitivo, gochujang
paste and grapefruit soda.

Not only do these cocktails taste
delightful, but they also look sensational.
Each chapter artfully weaves together
gorgeous photography inspired by
fashion, design and vintage art with the
beauty of the drinks themselves. And
Gabriel will have you smiling before your
drink is even ready with his anecdotes
about hazy beach days, sunsets over
Mexico City, the wild nights of his 20s and
his on-point pop culture references.
    Mood Drinks is a stunning combination
of simple and unique alcohol-free
cocktails with fashion-inspired visuals
and light-hearted humor that come
together to make a beautiful book worthy
of both your coffee table and bar cart.

MOOD DRINKS

Alcohol-Free Cocktails to Create the Perfect Mood

Gabriel Cabrera

Mood Drinks

appetite
by RANDOM HOUSE

Appetite by Random House® and colophon are
registered trademarks of Penguin Random House
LLC.

Library and Archives Canada Cataloguing in
Publication is available upon request.

ISBN: 978-0-525-61127-1
eBook ISBN: 978-0-525-61128-8

Photography by Gabriel Cabrera
Book and cover design by Jennifer Griffiths
Typeset by Sean Tai

Printed in China

Published in Canada by Appetite by Random
House®, a division of Penguin Random House
Canada Limited.

www.penguinrandomhouse.ca

10 9 8 7 6 5 4 3 2 1

appetite   Penguin
by RANDOM HOUSE   Random House
                  Canada

To mom and dad for their
never-ending love and support.

Para mamá y papá,
su amor y apoyo eterno.

1 ............INTRODUCTION

4 ....WHAT ARE MOOD DRINKS?

7 ....GLOSSARY

15 ....GETTING IN THE MOOD

PG 29

CH.1 CHILL

BITTER / SMOKY / COZY

22 ....SMOKING GUNS & ROSES

24 ....ECHINACEA TRANCE

27 ....HAZY SUNSET

29 ....I'M NOT YOUR BABY

30 ....FIRE AND GRASS

33 ....BITTER SODA FLOAT

34 ....APPLE OF MY EYE

34 ....COJICHA

35 ....FLORAL COZIES

39 ....HALVACHATA

40 ....SLEEPY CHERRIES

42 ....UMBRELLA BELLA

45 ....SESAME BLANKET

47 ....CRANDELION

48 ....BITTER DUSK

PG 54

CH.2 UPLIFT

SAVORY / SPICY / FIZZY

54 ....GOLDEN HOUR

57 ....ALOE, MONTREAL?

58 ....JAZU!

61 ....RITA ROCKS

62 ....THE DIRRRTY ONE

64 ....SHISO CUKE SOUR

66 ....CHAVELA

66 ....THAI BASIL FIZZ SODA

67 ....MARGALOMA FLOAT

70 ....GUAVA BRAVA

72 ....CELERY SODA

75 ....COCOAMOCO SELTZER

77 ....GREEN COCONUTS

78 ....WALNUT CHAI DOS LECHES

80 ....FLAMING MARY

PG 88

CH.3 CELEBRATE

CITRUS / FLORAL / FRUIT-FORWARD

86..........OH MY GLÖGG
88..........GINGER GLAM
91..........APASIONADO
92..........FOUNTAIN OF BEAUTY
95..........GRANNY'S FAVE
96..........SMOOTH WATERMELON
98..........PEAR CINNAMON HEARTS
98..........KARAT GOLD

99..........POMEGRANATE SOUR
102........LA FLOR
105........MANGO TANGO
106........LYCHEE LOCA
109........PINEAPPLE JASMINE CUP
110........A SHOT OF JOY
112........THE GLOW

PG 130

CH.4 EXPLORE

FUNKY / FERMENTED / ODDBALL

118........GRAPE STALLION
121........PLUM BLOSSOM SHRUB
122........GO BANANAS
124........SAGE AWAY
127........RHUBARBARA
128........TEPACHE PUNCH
130........THE EVERGREEN
131........PURPLE CLOUDS

131........WOODY BOOCH
135........UMAMILADA
136........PICKLED COOLER
138........NUTTYRATO
141........GOCHU SODA
143........TINGLY CUKES
144........OIL PAINTING

147........ACKNOWLEDGMENTS
148........INDEX

INTRODUCTION

Dear reader, I am so happy you picked up this book! I am very excited to get in the mood with you and make a drink or two. But before we get all moody, let me tell you a bit about myself, my journey and how I came about this idea of mood drinks.

I was born in Teotihuacán, the famous town and archaeological site in the heart of Mexico. Living there meant I was always surrounded by culture, beautiful, rugged landscapes and lots of food. There was no escaping the magical pull of this place. My parents would go for their morning jog around the Pyramid of the Sun and I would play in the nearby ruins. It sounds wild, doesn't it? It definitely was a magical time and place.

Our family has been in that area for generations. Sometime back in 1906, one of our great-great ancestors opened a restaurant inside a grotto, right next to the archaeological site. This unique spot was a place of celebration, good food and gatherings. When I was a child, the restaurant was one of our favorite places to hang out. I still remember the cool dampness of the grotto (which was a blessing during scorching hot days in the summer) and the wilderness around it.

I experienced my first mood-related drink in this place. After playing, we would sit at the table to enjoy a cold drink. Adults were served margaritas or micheladas, and kids would get horchatas or agua de jamaica (cold hibiscus tea). Snacks would make their way to the table. It was a time to pause, cool off and reset. It was a ritual of coming together, to create a calm, relaxed mood.

In that memory of mine at the family restaurant, the key elements that built the mood were the company, the incredible space (we were all eating in a grotto, hello!) and the delicious cooling drinks. It's the last that interests me the most in this book, as a catalyst for both interaction and introspection.

Can a drink be more than a party favor? Can a drink, combined with the right elements, put us in a desired mood? To answer those questions I created this book! To go beyond the glass and into our mood. To think about using drinks to create the right atmosphere: to enhance our joy, celebrate our friendships, bring comfort when we need it and help us discover new ways of being.

You could say that this is my manifesto: to create a new way of drinking, where we sip concoctions that not only look beautiful and taste delicious but also enhance our overall mood. Where we are conscious and intentional about the ingredients we use, the spaces we inhabit, the people we invite into our lives. It's about being mindful, but also nonchalant. And above all, it's about feeling alive.

Let me tell ya, it's a mood!

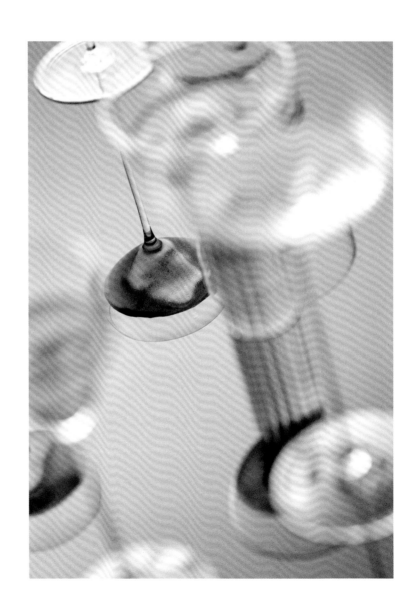

WHAT ARE MOOD DRINKS?

Remember those mood rings we used to have as kids? (Or as adults—no shame here.) The color-changing rock on the ring would inform its wearer of their mood. Was the rock turning blue? Then you were totally chill. What if it went black? Uh-oh, then you actually *needed* to chill.

I used a similar methodology to create this book, but instead of a color-changing rock, we use your mood as the compass. The mood you want to create is the goal, and a perfectly paired drink will help you get there.

I have categorized the drinks into four chapters led by mood and the flavor profiles I associate with that mood. This way you can find a drink according to your mood, but also according to your taste. Once you get good at identifying and building a mood, you can totally mix and match the recipes as you wish. It would be fun to discover what would happen when you serve both chill and uplift drinks at your next gathering. What kind of interaction and moods would result? I'm intrigued!

As you may already have noticed, the intention of this book is to be more mindful of what we do, and drinks are our way to bring this intention forward. Being able to identify the mood we are in, or the mood we want to create, and make a recipe based on that takes a bit of practice! But once you understand the concept, it becomes second nature. Hopefully, this practice of building the mood will spill beyond your drink and into other aspects of your life. Cheers to a well-balanced mood!

IN THE MOOD FOR WHAT?

So what do you drink when you are in the mood? "In the mood for what?" you may ask. To which I say, "In the mood to chill, uplift, celebrate, explore and everything else in between!" In this book you'll find a drink for every mood and occasion. Take a peek and find your drink!

Chapter 1:
Chill: Bitter, Smoky, Cozy
In this chapter you will find warm fuzzies, toasty treats and sips with depth are all included. These drinks are an excellent companion for when you're in the mood to relax and reset.

Chapter 2:
Uplift: Savory, Spicy, Fizzy
This chapter is devoted to drinks that give you a boost. The boost comes by way of salt, spices, veggies and more. I like to say that these drinks have a nice bite. These drinks are all about giving yourself a jolt of energy; they work as a delicious nudge.

Chapter 3:
Celebrate: Citrus, Floral, Fruit-Forward
This chapter is full of drinks with lots of color, personality and sparkle. These sips are perfect for when you're in the mood to celebrate with yourself or with friends and family. Perfect for one or for a gathering.

Chapter 4:
Explore: Funky, Fermented, Oddball
This chapter has deliciously funky-tasting stuff like shrubs, herbaceous tonics, fermented drinks and slightly more complex recipes. These drinks are perfect for when you're kinda tired of the same things and want to find a new sip.

CHILL PG 20

UPLIFT PG 52

CELEBRATE PG 84

EXPLORE PG 116

GLOSSARY

One of the goals I have for this book is for you to create drinks without the need for crazy equipment or ingredients. Most of the recipes here can be made with things you already have in your kitchen. Just in case you need a little guidance, though, here are some of my favorite tools, vessels and ingredient suggestions:

TOOLS
To make the recipes in this book, you'll need tools to stir, strain, blend and infuse. Here's a list that will get you covered:

Bar spoon: Really helpful to stir and mix drinks, especially tall drinks with lots of ice. Also perfect to help you slowly pour club soda or other fizzy add-ins without losing carbonation.

Blender: Any blender works for the recipes in this book. Just make sure it can crush ice.

Cocktail mixing glass: This works great to blend liquids, mash ingredients and stir any drink. You can use a bar mixing glass, or make do with a large, wide glass jar. You'll see some recipes ask you to "dry shake" ingredients, this just means to shake without ice, as it helps foam to form.

Cocktail shaker: My personal choice is a classic glass and metal shaker with a rubber edge. It's super easy to maneuver, it never leaks and it allows you to make more than one drink at a time. You can find this kind of shaker online or at any bartender supply store.

Glass jars: I use glass jars (mason or similar) to infuse, steep and keep my syrups and other concentrates. Glass jars are easy to clean and can be reused.

Jigger: For measuring liquids, I suggest you get a jigger from a bartender supply store (or order a good one online). Get one made out of stainless steel with marked measurements; this way you only need one to make almost any drink.

Measuring spoons and cups: I have one set of measuring cups (stainless steel) to get all my drinks done. I suggest avoiding plastic, as it can stain or retain flavors from random ingredients.

Nut milk bag: Some of the recipes here require straining through a nut milk bag. This is to ensure the liquid is as smooth as possible and no solids pass through.

Strainer: A fine-mesh strainer is also used for straining in the recipes and is an excellent tool to keep on hand.

VESSELS
In the recipes, I suggest which vessels work best for particular drinks, but here's a general list of vessels that will work for almost any drink in this book:

Cozy drinking bowls: I didn't use any ceramic bowls in this book (because you need to see the drinks in the photos), but I highly recommend that you do! Sipping a drink out of a ceramic bowl is the coziest thing you can do.

Fancy glassware: Think of coupes, flutes and anything with a stem. These are for drinks that like to get more attention, and for special occasions.

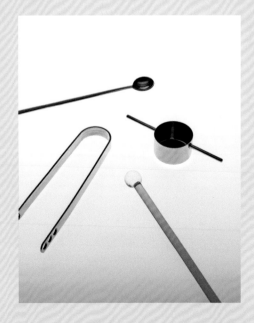

Short, shot-like glassware: For small but powerful drinks. Vintage liqueur glasses, shot glasses and small bistro-style glassware fall within this category.

Short, wide-mouth glassware: Anything short, like 2 to 4 inches tall, is good. This glassware is meant to be held in the hand and is perfect for slow or strong-flavored sips.

Tall glassware: Any tall and skinny glassware of your liking—even stemless champagne flutes work! These glasses are for drinks that have more liquid, fizz or elaborate garnish.

INGREDIENTS

As my gift to you, I made the recipes in this book with ingredients I had in my pantry and fridge—ones that you can easily find at a local shop or online. Here are some of the main ones you will see in the recipes:

Bitters: Most bitters are alcohol-based, but since they are used in very small quantities, their alcohol content is negligible by the time they are mixed in a drink. However, if you want to fully avoid all alcohol content, non-alcoholic bitter solutions are available online and at bartender supply stores. Both versions of bitters come in a variety of flavors. In this book I use lots of alcohol- and non-alcohol-based bitters to create the flavor profiles needed for the recipes. Bitters bring balance to a drink! Feel free to use the kind that best suits your needs.

Cocktail foamers: I really try to avoid using egg whites in drinks because once you remove the alcohol, egg white foam gives the drink a bit of a wet dog smell. Some people use aquafaba, but I tend to get mixed results with it. Fortunately, you can now find vegan or no-egg foamers in many forms. Most bartender supply stores carry them now, and you can find them easily online. As a general rule, a ¼ teaspoon of foamer per single drink will do the trick, but always check the label as each foamer is different—some may be a little less concentrated and require a larger quantity.

Ice: A quintessential ingredient for most cocktails! I'm a big fan of using ice from the store, the classic ice that comes in a bag, no fuss, no muss and always available. Store-bought ice has the perfect shape and size to make any drink: crushed, blended or stirred. For fancy cocktails, I recommend buying a couple of ice trays to make big ice cubes in different shapes; spheres and large cubes are the usual suspects. These trays are also perfect to make fun ice cubes with things in them like edible flowers, spices and other aromatics to complement your drinks. I always keep a few trays of fancy ice in my freezer so it's ready when I need it.

Salts: Salt is used quite a bit throughout this book. It brings balance and gives depth to almost any drink. My preferred type of salt is sea salt (as called for in many of the recipes); if no specific type is mentioned, use whatever salt you have on hand (kosher, flaky sea salt, Himalayan, etc.). When salt is used to rim the glass of a drink, I will also mention what kind of liquid you should use (e.g., lemon or lime juice). If there's no liquid ingredient mentioned in the recipe, a simple dip in water will do. To rim a glass, just dip it in the liquid, then dip it in salt and you're good to go.

Smoking ingredients: There are a few recipes that require beginner smoking, but don't worry, you don't need to buy those crazy cocktail smoking guns—I offer a super DIY method that works just as well. I recommend using applewood chips, since they're available at any hardware store (in the barbecue section) and online. Applewood chips are also super easy to handle, and their size makes them perfect for beginner use at home. If you don't want to use wood chips, you can always burn dried herbs. Remember to never, ever set an ingredient on fire and walk away! Always make sure to put out any flames and be safe. It's the smoke we're after, not the flame.

Spices: Most of the spices in this book are probably already in your pantry, and those that aren't can be easily purchased online or at your local grocery store. I'm excited for you to discover your own drink spice mixes! Feel free to experiment.

Syrups: You can make a simple syrup with a 1:1 ratio of sugar and water. To make it, in a small pot, mix 1 cup sugar (granulated or brown) and 1 cup water. Place over medium-low heat and stir until the sugar dissolves. Remove from the heat and let cool. You can store any leftovers in a glass container in the fridge for up to 2 weeks.

Once you get the hang of making simple syrup, you can play with the ratio of water to sugar to increase or decrease sweetness. You can also use different kinds of sugar (brown, coconut, pure cane, etc.) to obtain different tastes. Ready-made simple syrups are available to buy at any bartender supply store—or you can use flavored syrups available at coffee shops or in the soda section at the grocery store.

Teas: This book uses a lot of teas to get that nice bite from their tannins. To get the best tea, I go to my local tea shop, where they can guide me through my selections. In a pinch, just go to your grocery store and use whatever they have available. The goal is to steep the tea long enough to develop the tannins we need for the drink. One cool tip I recommend is to cover your tea while it steeps so that all the aromatic oils stay within the liquid.

Other specialty ingredients: For many specialty ingredients, I visit Asian markets, Latin stores and bodegas. Get out there and explore your city! Find new local shops that carry products not available at big-box grocery stores. A lot of things can be ordered online too.

NON-ALCOHOLIC SPIRITS AND OTHER ALTERNATIVES

I thought it would be helpful to include information about non-alcoholic spirits and other non-alcoholic alternatives, since some of the recipes in this book call for them. The market for non-alcoholic alternatives has exploded in the last couple of years, and there will probably be even more of them by the time this book

comes out. That's a good thing! But with such variety comes the obvious question: Which one to choose? Here are some of the favorite staples in my mood nook (more about that on p. 15):

Acid-based: These are mixes derived from fruits or non-alcoholic wines. They are perfect for shrubs and anything that requires a touch of high acidity. Lots of wineries and breweries are making them now. Think of this flavor profile as a high-acidity natural wine, sour beer or tangy liqueur, but with none of the alcohol.

Aperitivo-style: These usually have an Italian aperitivo-inspired flavor profile—anything with deeply bitter flavor notes and a touch of sweetness. These tend to be more spice-forward than fruity. They're great to add to a variety of drinks, and some can be enjoyed on their own (they're quite strong, but delicious). Think of this flavor profile as a non-alcoholic Campari or Aperol.

Distilled, infused water-based spirits: Several brands now carry water that has been infused with spices—similar to how it's done for liquor, but zero proof. These water-based mixes are very subtle, so they are better for minimal sips (think mixer and soda water or mellow-flavored ingredients). The flavor profile of alternative zero-proof spirits is similar to gin, vodka, mezcal or tequila.

Wellness elixir spirits and functional concentrates: These non-alcoholic mixers fall on the wellness side of things. These are any elixirs that have added ingredients like mushrooms, herbal tinctures, collagen, seaweed, and more. I aways love a drink with a perk! My favorite wellness elixir–style mixes are mushroom-based; they have a deep earthy flavor that's very umami. Others have a lovely floral aftertaste. Think of this flavor profile as zero-proof fortified wines (like vermouth) and heavy liqueurs (like Bénédictine).

GETTING IN THE MOOD

We've talked about how mood drinks work and how you can use the book chapters to find your best drink pairing. Before we fully jump into the recipes, let's talk about getting in the mood and setting the scene.

Though getting in the mood has obvious cheeky connotations, I mean this more in a general sense of creating the perfect ambience that matches whatever mood you're going for with your drink. There's more to setting a scene or mood than simply sipping on a drink. The place you are in, the glass or cup you use, the music you play, the lighting you use and even the scent of your space are all important to creating the right mood.

You probably have most of the stuff you need; you may just need to rearrange a few things or add a couple of details. Don't think that you need to do some crazy shopping spree or reno your space to create a mood. That's not it! The goal here is to make time and space for yourself with what you already have. Obviously if you find something cute that you want to add to your mood-building routine, by all means go for it—this isn't about restriction! This is about mindfulness, connection and enjoyment.

To make it easy for you to set the scene, I've broken down each mood into space, objects and atmosphere at the start of each chapter (see pp. 20, 52, 84 and 116). Take this as your starting point, as a way for you to experiment and find out what you truly like—and what helps get you in the mood.

—

THE MOOD NOOK

The mood nook is the area that's allocated to making your mood. Think of it as the equivalent of a bar cart, except there's more than bottles and glassware. The mood nook is where you keep your vessels, mixers (if they don't require refrigeration), scents and other tools to get you in the mood.

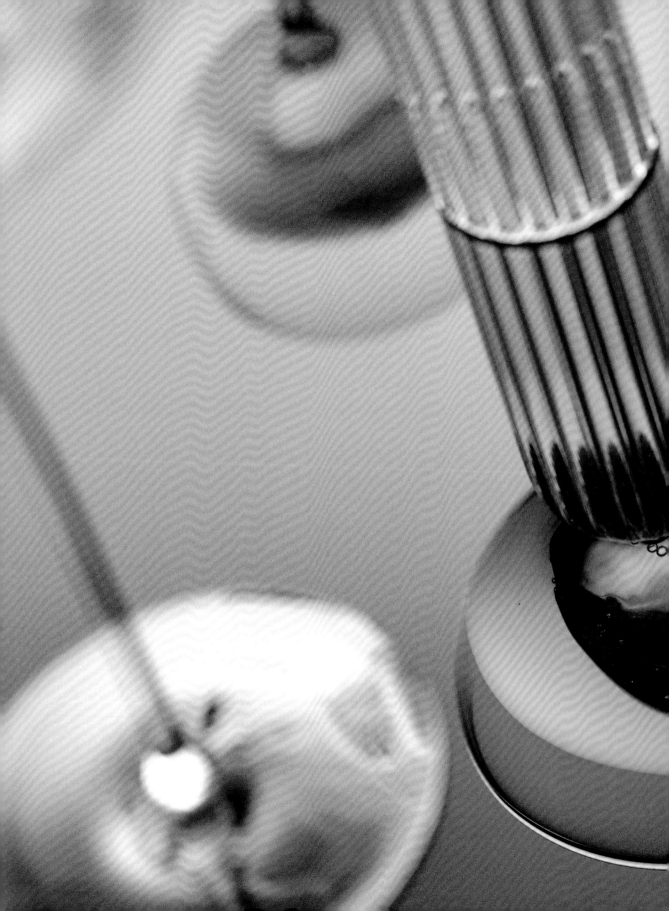

Chill

22 .... SMOKING GUNS & ROSES

24 .... ECHINACEA TRANCE

27 .... HAZY SUNSET

29 .... I'M NOT YOUR BABY

30 .... FIRE AND GRASS

33 .... BITTER SODA FLOAT

34 .... APPLE OF MY EYE

34 .... COJICHA

35 .... FLORAL COZIES

39 .... HALVACHATA

40 .... SLEEPY CHERRIES

42 .... UMBRELLA BELLA

45 .... SESAME BLANKET

47 .... CRANDELION

48 .... BITTER DUSK

Bitter
Smoky
Cozy

SETTING THE MOOD TO

CHILL

To chill is to create a relaxed, low-key and carefree atmosphere. It's about the essentials only—essentials that are conducive to slowing down, and being with ourselves.

SPACE

To set your space for a chill mood, start with an organized, clean area. Clutter calls for more clutter, and we want the opposite of this. We want a space that, for however long we are in it, allows us to disconnect and not think about chores like dirty laundry, dishes or anything else. If you want to have a chill moment, plan ahead and do all your house duties in advance so that when the time comes, you do nothing more than relax.

The location you choose to chill is also important: Is it on your couch? In your bedroom? By a fire? You don't need anything grand so long as it feels right for you. My favorite space to chill is the corner of my couch at home, where I can snuggle without care, where my side table is nearby so I can put my drink down. Very little effort is needed to get in the mood in this spot!

OBJECTS

Go for curves, soft textures and subtle colors. Unlike what people say, size does matter. For instance, a mug that's big enough to wrap your hands around feels way cozier than something tiny like, say, an espresso cup, which is meant to be used for a very short time (you shoot back the espresso and move on). The same applies to glassware: wide-mouth glassware is perfect for this mood. You can play with the height of the glass and see what feels better in your hand. Tall and wide like a coupe? Or short and wide like an old-fashioned glass?

In terms of materials, anything with a tactile quality is great! Think of unglazed ceramics, etched glassware and porcelain. You want a bit of texture, something that makes your sense of touch wander and explore. This is what helps you to disconnect and chill.

My favorite cup at home is made out of clay, and I bought it in Oaxaca, Mexico. It has a soft, round profile and it's quite chunky. This is my official "it's time to relax" cup.

ATMOSPHERE

To create a chill atmosphere, you'll need the right lighting, good tunes and a bit of scent to seal the deal. For light, choose low-profile warm lighting, candles or natural window light whenever possible. The goal here is to have a soft and warm vibe enveloping the scene. Low light allows your brain to chill, and it tells your other senses that it's time to kick back and relax. Think also of ways that you can diffuse the light. If you have a lamp right next to you, the glare might bother you and you won't be able to get in the mood. Try simply putting the lamp down on the floor, and voilà! Low-profile, diffused light on demand.

The last component here, and one of my favorites, is scent. Scent is a very personal choice, so you have to figure out what feels right for you. Some people really can't chill when there's a strong scent in the room, while others slow down by smelling something they love, like incense or a scented candle. For me, anything with a deep scent profile and layers is perfect; something related to nature, like wood, the ocean or smoke. If you prefer an environment that is scent-free, open your windows and let the air flow! A fresh breeze will do wonders to build your mood.

SMOKING GUNS N' ROSES

MAKES 1

This drink serves 90s core memories like no other. It's a good one to enjoy while you go down memory lane, daydreaming of your grunge days. Do you ever have a guilty-pleasures night when you listen to your favorite songs from growing up? It's the best thing to put you in a nostalgic mood! I say, take out your old CDs (if you still have them), make yourself this drink and blast that music!

Cocktail
½ cup flat tonic water (stir tonic water for about 1 minute to get rid of most of the fizz)

1 tbsp freshly squeezed lemon juice

1 dash rose water

5 dashes smoke and oak bitters or non-alcoholic bitters of choice

1 tbsp simple syrup (see p. 12)

¼ tsp cocktail foamer (see p. 11)

Ice

1 edible rose petal, to garnish (optional)

To Smoke the Cocktail
Baking sheet

1 wood chip (applewood is the easiest to find and works great!)

Small pot

01 **Cocktail:** Place the tonic water, lemon juice, rose water, bitters, simple syrup and cocktail foamer in a shaker and dry shake for about 1 minute. Add the ice and shake vigorously until the shaker is frosty, about 2 minutes. Strain the contents into a nice glass of your liking.

02 **To Smoke:** Place the glass on the baking sheet. Light up the wood chip and let it smoke, placing it right next to the drink. Cover both the glass and the wood chip with a small pot and let the drink mingle with the smoke for a couple of minutes.

03 Remove the pot, garnish the drink with a rose petal and serve.

ECHINACEA TRANCE

MAKES 1

You may think to yourself, "What the heck is echinacea doing in a drink?" And I agree with you. When I first thought of this drink, I was like, "Are people going to hate this?" But I love the bitter—and subtly floral—taste of echinacea, so here it is! Please share with me on social media if you love it or hate it. (Just make sure you are totally fine with sipping echinacea first, as some people are allergic to it.)

Super-Steeped Echinacea Tea
3 bags echinacea tea
⅓ cup hot water

Cocktail
Ice, plus 1 big ice cube to serve
¼ cup non-alcoholic gin (see p. 12)
¼ cup super-steeped echinacea tea (above)
1 tsp brown sugar
1 dash Angostura or aromatic bitters
Lemon peel, to garnish

01 **Super-Steeped Echinacea Tea:** Place the tea bags in the hot water and let steep for at least 15 minutes. Remove the tea bags and use the tea immediately. Save leftover tea for another cocktail; it'll keep in the fridge for 1 week.

02 **Cocktail:** In a mixing glass with ice, stir the non-alcoholic gin, super-steeped tea and brown sugar until the sugar dissolves. Strain into a glass with a big ice cube. Add a dash of bitters on top, garnish with lemon peel and serve.

HAZY SUNSET

MAKES 1

You know when you're in the height of summer and you're coming back home after a long day of fun? You can see a bit of haze in the sky from the heat, and you just plop on your couch exhausted but full of bliss? My favorite kind of feeling! I tried to recreate that blissful "just gonna plop on the couch after a hot, fun day" vibe with this drink. It's a slow sipper, so take your time and enjoy.

½ cup cold apricot juice

¼ tsp almond extract

1 tbsp freshly squeezed lemon juice

1 tsp smoky bitters or non-alcoholic bitters of
   choice, plus more to taste

2 pinches sea salt

Ice

01   Place all ingredients in a mixing glass with some ice and swirl to combine until the glass is frosty. Strain into a glass with fresh ice and serve.

I'M NOT YOUR BABY

MAKES 1

Remember that life-changing experience called *The Devil Wears Prada*? There's a scene in the movie toward the end when Anne Hathaway's character, Andy, drops the iconic line "I'm not your baby" to tell her shady lover that she's not impressed with his behavior. This scene is part of the aftermath of a night out fueled by lots of red wine.

I want us to feel a bit of Andy's fantasy life at home, with a glass in hand full of delicious-tasting tannins but none of the shadiness or hangover. Feel free to play around with the ratios and make it your own, because just like Andy said to Miranda Priestly, we are all learning about "this stuff."

NOTE
To burn the dried orange slice, carefully torch it until it smokes a little.

Ice

⅓ cup non-alcoholic aperitivo-style mixer (see p. 12), chilled

¼ cup blackberry juice, chilled

1 dash aromatic bitters

Burnt dried orange slice, to garnish (see note; optional)

01 In a mixing glass with ice, stir the non-alcoholic mixer and blackberry juice until the glass is frosty. Strain into a fancy glass, add the dash of aromatic bitters and garnish with burnt orange.

FIRE AND GRASS

This drink reminds me of camping, which I did once in my life and totally hated. But then I discovered something better—glamping! And that was totally fine with me ☺. Regardless of the style, we can all agree that core memories of camping always involve some kind of bonfire, so here I bring some of that coziness into a glass.

Super-Steeped Bergamot Tea
3 bags bergamot tea

½ cup hot water

Cocktail
1 small piece fresh lemongrass, plus more to garnish

1 tbsp brown sugar

½ cup super-steeped bergamot tea (above), cooled

3 drops orange blossom water (optional)

Ice

Cold seltzer, to top

To Smoke the Cocktail
Baking sheet

1 wood chip for smoking (applewood is the easiest to find and works great!)

Small pot

01 **Super-Steeped Bergamot Tea:** Place the tea bags in the hot water and let steep for 15 minutes. Remove the tea bags and let cool for a few minutes.

02 **Cocktail:** In a mixing glass, combine the fresh lemongrass and brown sugar and gently muddle until the sugar is dissolved. Add the cooled steeped tea and orange blossom water, and stir to combine.

03 Strain the contents into a tall glass filled with ice and top with cold seltzer.

04 **To Smoke:** Place the glass on the baking sheet. Light up the wood chip and let it smoke, placing it right next to the drink. Cover both the glass and the wood chip with a small pot and let the drink mingle with the smoke for a couple of minutes.

05 Remove the pot, garnish the drink with lemongrass and enjoy.

BITTER SODA FLOAT

MAKES 1

Who doesn't like a float? Especially when it's an upgraded version like this one. For this drink we use a bitter soda, like chinotto, Stappi, BIBI or similar. These sodas are good on their own, but when you mix them with sorbet and put them in a nice glass, they go to the next level of fun and yum.

Ice

1 tbsp freshly squeezed lemon juice

1 tsp vanilla extract

1 can bitter soda of your liking
(see recipe introduction)

2 to 3 small scoops grapefruit sorbet, or lime or lemon sorbet if you can't find grapefruit

Grapefruit peel, to garnish

01   Fill a glass with ice and add the lemon juice and vanilla. Pour in the bitter soda to fill the glass about two-thirds full.

02   Gently scoop the grapefruit sorbet into the glass. Garnish with fresh grapefruit peel.

1

APPLE OF MY EYE

MAKES 1

Sometimes you need to feel yourself, you know? You wanna give yourself some much-needed love and affection. In a way, you become the apple of your own eye! How cute. I love having this drink when I am ready to disconnect from the world for some quality me time. For this recipe, you want to super-steep the black tea (I love regular Earl Grey)—this brings out a bit of bitterness and lets the tannins really come through. It's super good!

Super-Steeped Black Tea

3 bags black tea

½ cup hot water

Cocktail

¼ cup super-steeped black tea (above), cooled

¼ cup good-quality apple cider

½ tsp apple cider vinegar

¼ tsp orange bitters or aromatic bitters

1 tsp maple syrup

Handful of ice

01 **Super-Steeped Black Tea:** Place the tea bags in the hot water and let steep for 10 to 15 minutes. Remove tea bags and let cool.

02 **Cocktail:** Place all ingredients in a mixing glass. Stir for 1 minute, until the glass is frosty. Strain contents into a small, short glass.

2

COJICHA

MAKES 1

A creamy, velvety take on a dirty hojicha. What's that, you ask? It's hojicha tea, milk and coffee. Hojicha is a type of Japanese green tea that has been toasted, so it has this amazingly cozy, deep, rich nutty, earthy flavor. For this extra-chill version, I added a touch of coconut milk plus brown rice syrup and vanilla, which turn it into an instant warm hug.

1 tsp hojicha tea powder

¼ cup warm water

½ tsp vanilla extract

1 tsp brown rice syrup or ½ tsp brown sugar

¼ cup oat milk or milk of choice

¼ cup coconut milk

1 shot decaf espresso or 1 tsp decaf instant coffee

01 In a small bowl or a wide-mouth cup, whisk the hojicha tea in the water until dissolved. Add the vanilla and brown rice syrup and stir to combine. Steam (or heat on the stove) the oat and coconut milks and pour over the tea mixture. Top with a shot of espresso and serve.

NOTE
You can enjoy this recipe hot or cold depending on your mood. If you want to serve it cold, follow the same steps above, but pour the entire mixture into a glass filled with ice.

3

FLORAL COZIES

MAKES 1

Remember those floral crochet blankets that our grannies used to have? They were so cozy and cute! That's exactly what this drink is: a delicious, slow-sipping, cozy, floral moment. It gets bonus points because it also happens to look glamorous and rich, like one of those drinks people have when they own the place. So go ahead, own it, sip it and cozy up.

Super-Steeped Chamomile, Lavender and Grapefruit Infusion

3 bags chamomile tea or
   chrysanthemum tea

2 tsp dried lavender

1 inch grapefruit peel

½ cup hot water

Cocktail

½ cup super-steeped chamomile, lavender
   and grapefruit infusion (above)

½ tsp vanilla extract

1 tsp brown sugar

¼ cup aloe vera juice

1 dash Angostura or aromatic bitters

2 large ice cubes

Grapefruit peel, to garnish

01   **Super-Steeped Chamomile, Lavender and Grapefruit Infusion:** Place the tea bags, dried lavender and grapefruit peel in the hot water and let steep for 20 minutes. Remove tea bags, strain and let cool.

02   **Cocktail:** Place the infusion, vanilla, sugar, aloe vera juice and bitters in a glass with 1 large ice cube. Stir to combine until the sugar dissolves.

03   Strain into a wide-mouth glass with a fresh big ice cube. Garnish with the grapefruit peel and serve.

3-FLORAL COZIES

2-COJICHA

1-APPLE OF MY EYE

RECIPES ON PG 34-35

HALVACHATA

MAKES 1

Are you obsessed with halva? I kinda am. It all started a long, long time ago in a far, far away galaxy called the Chelsea Market in New York City, where I tried a pistachio and rose halva. The mix of slightly bitter, sweet and fragrant layers totally blew my mind. I've been hooked ever since! I obviously wanted to insert a bit of Mexican magic with a touch of horchata-ish flavorings. This is definitely a cozy drink to slowly sip away, like a liquid dessert.

2 tbsp halva, any flavor you like (I like simple vanilla)

1 cinnamon stick

½ tsp vanilla extract

1 cup rice milk

1 tbsp orgeat syrup

1 big ice cube

Shaved cinnamon and nutmeg, to top

01 Place the halva, cinnamon stick, vanilla extract, rice milk and orgeat into a blender. Blend on high speed for about 2 minutes, until the halva and cinnamon sticks have been crushed.

02 Pour into a wide-mouth glass with the big ice cube. Top with shaved cinnamon and nutmeg.

SLEEPY CHERRIES

MAKES 1

Tart, spiced and with a touch of bitterness. I read in some health magazine a while ago that having a glass of cherry juice at night could help you sleep better. I remember thinking to myself, "A treat before bed? Sign me up!" However, the thought of spilling the juice on my bed (making it look more like a crime scene and less like a sleep sanctuary) made me think twice. I figured I would turn cherry juice into this delicious drink instead! A drink one can sip to unwind, somewhere out of bed.

NOTE
Natural cherry juice can be found in most health-food stores. Any natural cherry juice will do; just make sure it isn't artificially flavored.

1 cup tart natural cherry juice

1 tbsp freshly squeezed lemon juice

¼ tsp aromatic or orange bitters

2 cinnamon sticks

1 pinch freshly ground nutmeg

1 large piece orange peel
  (make sure to remove the pith)

Ice cubes

Sparkling water

1 fresh cherry, to top (if they're in season)

01   Place the cherry juice, lemon juice, bitters, cinnamon sticks, nutmeg and orange peel into a clean glass jar. Stir a couple of times, then let steep in the fridge overnight or for at least 4 hours.

02   To serve, fill a tall glass with lots of ice and strain the drink into the glass. Top with sparkling water. Add fresh cherries on top because, cute!

UMBRELLA BELLA

I'm not afraid to admit that I have a slight obsession with coconut. Anything and everything coconut I will eat, drink and probably marry. This coconut drink reminds me of enjoying a few sunny days by the beach, no cares in the world other than falling asleep under an umbrella. Is there anything more chill than that? Don't think so!

½ cup non-alcoholic gin

1 tbsp coconut syrup

1 tsp freshly squeezed lemon juice

1 tsp orange bitters

Handful of ice, plus more to serve

1 piece dried coconut, to garnish (optional)

01 Place the non-alcoholic gin, coconut syrup, lemon juice and bitters in a mixing glass with some ice and stir until combined.

02 Strain into a small glass over a few ice cubes. Garnish with dried coconut and serve.

SESAME BLANKET

The inspiration for this drink is salty licorice, which is a very popular candy in Nordic countries and a few others on that side of the pond. The first time I tried salty licorice was at a movie theater, and it took me by surprise. I was so confused! But also pleasantly surprised by the flavor combo.

Black licorice is a love-it-or-hate-it type of thing, so for this recipe I used black sesame milk with some spices that give a nod to the flavors in the candy, but in a milder and nuttier way. Honestly, this drink is very unique, and I'm excited for you to try it and make it your new favorite treat to chill.

Spiced Black Sesame Milk

½ cup black sesame seeds

1 cup warm water (for soaking)

3 cups water

2 cinnamon sticks

2 pinches salt

2 tbsp brown sugar

Cocktail

Lime or lemon wedge, to rim glass

1 tsp mixed sesame seeds

1 tsp fennel seeds, ground

1 pinch salt

1 cup spiced black sesame milk (above)

Ice, to serve (optional)

01 **Spiced Black Sesame Milk:** Soak the sesame seeds in the warm water for 30 minutes, then strain. Transfer the seeds to a blender, along with the 3 cups of water, and the cinnamon sticks, salt and brown sugar. Blend on high speed until smooth, about 2 or 3 minutes. Strain the contents through a nut milk bag placed over a clean bowl, squeezing the bag to get all the milk out. Pour the strained milk into a clean glass jar with a lid and seal. This will keep in the fridge for about 1 week.

02 **Cocktail:** Mix the sesame seeds, ground fennel seeds and salt together on a plate. Rim the glass with the lemon or lime wedge, then dip into the seeds. Pour the spiced black sesame milk into the glass. You can serve this at room temp or cold over ice.

CRANDELION

MAKES 1

The inspiration for this drink came from my young years as a party animal. There was a time in my life when I used to drink nothing but "budget-cosmos" (that's what I called the classic vodka cran cocktail). Now I like to reminisce about those wild days from home, relaxed on my couch with a book in hand. This drink has all the fun memories but none of the painful aftermath.

1 bag or 1 tbsp loose-leaf dandelion tea

¼ cup hot water

½ cup good cranberry juice

Splash of freshly squeezed orange juice

1 tbsp freshly squeezed lemon juice

¼ tsp cocktail foamer (see p. 11)

Ice

1 dash aromatic bitters

Fresh or dried edible dandelions, to garnish

01 Place the tea bag or leaves in the hot water and let steep for about 10 minutes. Let cool for a few minutes, then remove the tea bag (or strain if needed) and transfer to a shaker.

02 Add the cranberry juice, orange juice, lemon juice and cocktail foamer to the shaker. Dry shake for about 30 seconds first to get the foam going. Add the ice and shake again until the shaker gets frosty, about 1 minute.

03 Strain the drink into a wide-mouth glass or cup. Add the dash of bitters on top. Garnish with dandelions.

BITTER DUSK

MAKES 1

This drink came to me while I was watching the sunset from my place in Mexico City. The city haze makes the sky turn this wonderful, deep-red gradient. I find this kind of sunset to have a rather bittersweet feel: I am in awe of the colors and beauty of the moment, but I know it won't last long. I wanted to capture this moment of contemplation in a glass, where colors, feel and taste all mingle together.

Orange and Hibiscus Mix
Peel of 1 large orange
Peel of 1 lemon
½ cup hibiscus tea
2 cups water
1 cup granulated sugar

Cocktail
Ice
¼ cup orange and hibiscus mix (above)
2 dashes aromatic bitters
1 tbsp freshly squeezed lemon juice
Tonic water, to top
Orange peel or edible hibiscus flower, to garnish

01 **Orange and Hibiscus Mix:** Place all ingredients in a small saucepan over low heat and bring to a simmer. Simmer until the liquid has reduced by half. Let cool, then strain into a clean glass jar and place in the fridge. This will keep in the fridge for about 1 week.

02 **Cocktail:** In a tall glass filled with ice, combine the orange and hibiscus mix, bitters and lemon juice. Top with tonic water and garnish with an orange peel or edible hibiscus flower.

Uplift

54 .... GOLDEN HOUR

57 .... ALOE, MONTREAL?

58 .... JAZU!

61 .... RITA ROCKS

62 .... THE DIRRRTY ONE

64 .... SHISO CUKE SOUR

66 .... CHAVELA

66 .... THAI BASIL FIZZ SODA

67 .... MARGALOMA FLOAT

70 .... GUAVA BRAVA

72 .... CELERY SODA

75 .... COCOAMOCO SELTZER

77 .... GREEN COCONUTS

78 .... WALNUT CHAI DOS LECHES

80 .... FLAMING MARY

Spicy
Savory
Fizzy

SETTING THE MOOD

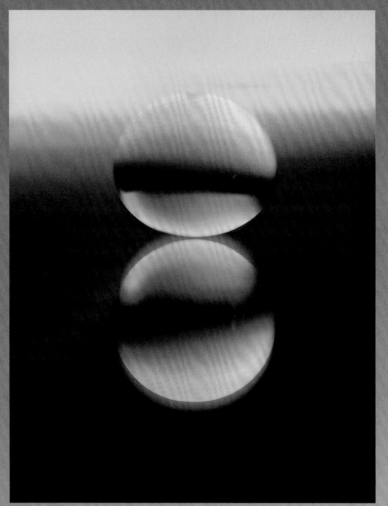

TO
UPLIFT

An uplifting mood is all about a boost of energy and happiness. It's the spark of a feel-good moment. It's a little pick-me-up!

SPACE

I would say this is the most flexible of the moods we explore in this book. Creating a pick-me-up mood is less about the location and more about making space for a moment to recharge, savor and get going. The space should be easy to access and not near anything that's too precious or delicate. It's about the ease of enjoyment.

OBJECTS

Since you want to spend most of your time enjoying the drink, keeping it simple is best. Use easy-to-clean surfaces, trays and tools, and glassware with clean, minimalist lines. Glass is the most obvious choice, but you can also use glazed ceramics (sturdy and stainless). Make it fun and use any vessel available to you, like bistro glassware, mismatched thrifted vessels and even regular water glasses.

Use color to boost the mood! Try colorful serving trays, a pop of color in the coasters or maybe a bright and cheerful glass. My favorite glass for when I'm ready to be uplifted is a bright pink cup that's sleek but very cheerful.

ATMOSPHERE

In the celebration section I mention using a light bulb that's bright and fun—here I suggest going for a bright cheerful color. Maybe make your lighting bright yellow or green. If you can't change the lighting, then use the color in the drink to bring that vibe.

The music you play here should be totally full of high energy. Think of it as a shot of something yummy to lift you up. You wouldn't play that music for hours on end, but it's good for a quick jolt of fun and joy. I suggest you make a playlist with your favorite one-hit wonders or the ride-or-die tunes that automatically get you in the mood.

For scent, you definitely want something strong. Something that tickles your senses and wakes you up. Think salty, hot and vibrant. My favorite choice for this mood is a tomato-scented candle (it's so fresh and energizing!) or a spritz of ginger-infused room scent. Remember that scent can come from the drink itself, so you don't have to spend too much time fussing around finding the perfect scent.

GOLDEN HOUR

The color of this drink is gorgeous and intense. It's like a sun bursting with heat, energy and joy. That's all packed into the ingredients as well—it was inspired by many wellness elixirs I've taken over the years, my favorite being turmeric and pepper. Health, color and happiness: What else could you ask from a drink?!

Turmeric Juice

3 cups water

2 small (½-inch) pieces fresh turmeric

Cocktail

1 cup non-alcoholic dry cider

1 tbsp turmeric juice (above)

½ tsp freshly ground black pepper
  (the finer the grind, the better)

1 tbsp freshly squeezed lemon juice

Crushed ice

1½ tbsp natural grenadine (avoid artificially flavored)

Fresh orange slice, to garnish

01 **Turmeric Juice:** Place the water and turmeric in a blender and blend on high for 1 minute. Strain into a clean airtight container. The juice will keep in the fridge for up to 1 week.

02 **Cocktail:** Gently stir the dry cider, turmeric juice, black pepper and lemon juice to combine.

03 Fill an old-fashioned glass with crushed ice and pour in the drink. Add the grenadine just before serving (it will sink and create a beautiful color gradient). Garnish with an orange slice.

ALOE, MONTREAL?

MAKES 1

Montreal steak spice is my secret weapon for this drink. It's savory and it packs a little peppery punch. I've seen it used in Caesar cocktails, and it adds such a nice bite. This flavor combo is different from a classic restaurant-style version, so I'm excited for you to try it at home!

Mint Concentrate

2 packed cups fresh mint

2 cups water

3 tbsp agave syrup

Cocktail

Ice

¼ cup mint concentrate (above), cooled

1 cup aloe juice

3 dashes aromatic bitters

1 tbsp freshly squeezed lime juice

Lime or lemon wedge, to rim glass

Montreal steak spice, to rim glass

Fresh mint, to garnish

01 **Mint Concentrate:** In a small saucepan, bring the mint, water and agave syrup to a simmer over low heat. Simmer for 15 minutes, then let cool. Strain the liquid and discard the mint. This will keep in a clean glass jar in the fridge for about 1 week.

02 **Cocktail:** Fill a shaker with ice. Add the mint concentrate, aloe juice, bitters and lime juice and shake until the shaker gets frosty.

03 Rim the glass of your choice with a lime or lemon wedge, then dip in the Montreal steak spice.

04 Strain the drink into the glass. Garnish with fresh mint and serve.

JAZU!

**MAKES 4 CUPS,
SERVES 4 TO 6**

This is such a fun drink and one of my favorites in this book. It came to be after I spent a few months in Mexico City doing recipe research. One day I went to the market to look for spices and fruits for testing, and I got a little bag of peeled jicama as a snack while shopping. As I was snacking away, a thought suddenly hit me: Wouldn't it be nice to have the flavor of this jicama as a drink?! I came back home to Vancouver and experimented mixing jicama with a few other things, but something was missing. The final key ingredient came to me as I was shopping at one of my favorite Japanese stores: yuzu soda! It was one of those aha moments. This drink has earthy, citrus and floral notes, which makes it quite unique!

NOTE
You can find yuzu juice online or in most Japanese markets or specialty bartender shops.

4 Granny Smith apples, cored and cut into cubes

1 medium jicama, peeled and cut into cubes

2½ tsp sea salt

2 tsp granulated sugar or 1 tbsp agave syrup

2 tsp freshly ground black pepper

1 tsp coriander seeds (optional)

¼ cup yuzu juice or freshly squeezed juice of ½ lime and ½ lemon

4 cups water

Ice

Green apple slice, to garnish

01 Place the apples, jicama, salt, sugar, pepper, coriander seeds, yuzu juice and water in a blender and blend on high for 2 to 3 minutes, until smooth. Once blended, refrigerate for about 1 hour to let the flavors infuse the water (you can just leave it in the blender container).

02 Strain through a fine-mesh strainer or nut milk bag into a clean container, making sure to squeeze all the liquid through. This is your Jazu!

03 Add some ice to your glass of choice, pour in some Jazu!, garnish with an apple slice and enjoy. You can keep any leftover Jazu! in a clean glass jar in the fridge for up to 3 days.

RITA ROCKS

This drink is extra!
So you better match
its energy.

Remember Pop Rocks? The super-fun candy that starts popping like crazy once you put it in your mouth? Wouldn't it be nice to experience that in a drink? Well, what baby wants, baby gets: Pop Rocks and a drink to go along with them! This is going to wake up your entire being.

Super-Steeped Green Tea
3 bags green tea
¼ cup hot water

Cocktail
1 lime wedge (to make the Pop Rocks "spoon")
1 package Pop Rocks candy
1 scoop lemon sorbet
¼ cup super-steeped green tea (above), cooled
5 dashes orange bitters
Juice of 1 lime
¼ tsp celery salt

01 **Super-Steeped Green Tea:** Place the tea bags in the hot water and let steep for 15 minutes. Remove the tea bags and let cool.

02 **Cocktail:** Gently remove the peel from the lime wedge. Place the Pop Rocks onto the peel. This is your Pop Rock spoon!

03 In a small bowl, combine the lemon sorbet, super-steeped green tea, bitters, lime juice and celery salt. Stir until the sorbet softens a bit, but don't let it melt, about 20 seconds.

04 Pour the mixture into a short glass. Serve with the Pop Rocks spoon on the side and enjoy.

THE DIRRRTY ONE

MAKES 1

You know that feeling when you bite into an olive? That savory, slightly sweet and briny spark of flavor? Yeah, I wanted to bring some of that feeling into this section of the book. In cocktail circles, anything with pickle juice seems to be called dirty, so why not follow that here? Let's have a little dirty fun of our own!

NOTE
I strongly suggest you blast Christina Aguilera's "Dirrty" while making this drink.

¼ cup good white grape juice (low sugar is best)

¼ cup non-alcoholic gin (see p. 12)

2 tsp olive brine (add more to make it filthy!)

½ tsp Angostura or aromatic bitters

Ice

Persian cucumber spear dipped in salt, to garnish

01 Place the white grape juice, non-alcoholic gin, olive brine and bitters in a mixing glass with ice. Stir until frosty. Strain the contents into a fancy coupe or similar glass. Garnish with a cucumber slice dipped in salt.

SHISO CUKE SOUR

I discovered shiso when I moved to Canada and tried sushi for the first time. I fell in love with its flavor and how well it pairs with savory food. For this drink we are combining its herbaceous flavor notes with cucumber and a little salt to bring out the most of it all. This drink is super fresh, so it's perfect for a night when you need to clear your mind and get stuff done.

NOTE
You can find fresh shiso in Japanese markets. If you can't find any, ask your local sushi shop if they could sell some to you (and make new friends!).

Cucumber Juice
1 long English cucumber
2 cups water
1 pinch salt

Shiso Syrup
2 cups water
1 cup granulated sugar
½ cup loosely packed fresh shiso leaves

Cocktail
½ cup cucumber juice (above)
2 tbsp freshly squeezed lemon juice
1 tbsp shiso syrup (above)
¼ tsp sea salt
1 tsp cocktail foamer (see p. 11)
Ice
Fresh shiso leaf, to garnish

01   **Cucumber Juice:** Peel the cucumber and cut it into chunks. Place in a blender, add the water and salt and blend until smooth. Strain through a fine-mesh strainer or nut milk bag into a clean airtight container. The juice will keep in the fridge for up to 4 days.

02   **Shiso Syrup:** In a pot, combine the water, sugar and shiso leaves and simmer over low heat for about 20 minutes, or until the mixture has reduced by half. Remove from heat and let cool. This syrup will keep in the fridge for up to 1 week.

03   **Cocktail:** Place the cucumber juice, lemon juice, shiso syrup, salt and cocktail foamer in a shaker and dry shake for about 1 minute. Add ice and shake again until the shaker gets frosty, about 2 minutes.

04   Strain into a sleek glass. Slap the fresh shiso leaf (this will release the aromatics) and use as a garnish.

1

CHAVELA

MAKES 1

The michelada is one of Mexico's most popular beer cocktails. It's usually prepared with beer, lime juice, spices and some kind of flavoring sauce (like Worcestershire). A michelada loaded with Clamato and next-level sauces (like chamoy or sriracha) is called a michelada preparada. This version is a close cousin of the original; it has no alcohol, but the same preparation. All the spices, fizz and savory notes will surely lift you up!

Celery salt, to rim glass

Lime wedges, to rim glass and garnish

Ice

¼ cup Clamato or V8-style juice

½ tsp Valentina hot sauce or similar

1 tsp Worcestershire sauce

2 tbsp freshly squeezed lime juice

1 tsp lime zest

1 non-alcoholic lager beer

Fresh oregano or parsley, to garnish (optional)

01 Place the celery salt on a plate. Rim the glass with a lime wedge, then dip into the celery salt to rim.

02 Fill a tall glass with ice and add the Clamato, hot sauce, Worcestershire, lime juice and zest. Swirl the ingredients with a bar spoon to combine. Slowly pour in the non-alcoholic beer to fill the glass. Garnish with a lime wedge and fresh oregano.

2

THAI BASIL FIZZ SODA

MAKES 1

Thai basil is a favorite herb of mine. Its flavor is different from regular basil, with more of a licorice and spice profile. When you combine it with citrus and fizz, you get an uplifting glass of joy. For this recipe, I add some of the strained mash back into the drink to get a bit of texture. If you don't like bits in your drink, skip this step.

Thai Basil Mash

2 tsp celery seeds

½ cup loosely packed fresh Thai basil

½ tsp salt

½ tsp pepper

Zest and juice of 4 limes

½ cup water

2-inch chunk of cucumber

Cocktail

¼ cup Thai basil mash (above)

1 tbsp brown sugar

1 tbsp freshly squeezed lime juice

Ice

Lime-infused soda (LaCroix or similar), to top

Fresh Thai basil, to garnish (optional)

01 **Thai Basil Mash:** Place all ingredients in a blender and blend until smooth. Strain through a fine-mesh strainer into a clean container. Add 1 or 2 tbsp of the strained mash back into the mixture for texture. This mash will keep in the fridge for up to 3 days.

02 **Cocktail:** Place the Thai basil mash, brown sugar and lime juice in a tall glass and stir until the sugar dissolves. Fill the glass with ice and top with lime-infused soda. Garnish with Thai basil and serve.

3

MARGALOMA FLOAT

MAKES 1

As you may have noticed, I really like floats and things with sorbet and ice cream. This time I'm taking one of my favorite drinks in a savory, ever-so-slightly spicy direction. The inspiration for this cocktail is a childhood memory of family gatherings with my aunties, who love a good paloma cocktail (tequila and grapefruit soda). The kids wouldn't get one, of course. Instead, we would get grapefruit soda with a lime sorbet float, which to me tastes almost the same. This drink is a merge of that one from my childhood plus some notes from a margarita—think citrus, savory and mouthwatering.

¼ cup super-steeped green tea (see p. 61), cooled

1 tbsp freshly squeezed lime juice

1 tsp Angostura or aromatic bitters

Canned grapefruit soda, to top

1 scoop lemon or lime sorbet

Tajín seasoning or similar, to garnish

01 Place the super-steeped green tea, lime juice and bitters in a glass and stir to combine. Top with grapefruit soda. Carefully add the scoop of sorbet, and sprinkle Tajín seasoning on top. Add a straw and serve.

GUAVA BRAVA

I feel guava is a bit of an underdog when it comes to drinks. It's such a delicious fruit! And I'm here to push my guava agenda—no shame. Since guava has such an intense flavor, you need only a few ingredients to make it shine. This sip is meant to be a little burst of flavor to perk you up; it has a bit of heat in it, so feel free to adjust it to suit your own taste.

½ cup guava nectar, cold
1 tbsp freshly squeezed lemon juice
½ tsp ume plum vinegar
1 pinch cayenne pepper
Ground sumac, to top

01 In a small container, stir the guava nectar, lemon juice, plum vinegar and cayenne pepper until combined.

02 Pour into a chilled small glass. Sprinkle sumac on top and serve.

CELERY SODA

For all you celery lovers out there, you are about to have a religious experience—of the vegetable kind. Is there anything more savory than the pure taste of celery? I don't think so. Celery is one of those deceiving vegetables that you don't think of as having a lot of flavor but is actually quite intense. This soda has lots of mineral, earthy notes that combine with green tea to make it super fresh and delicious.

Super-Steeped Green Tea

3 bags green tea

1 cup hot water

Cocktail

2 packed cups celery tops (it's okay to include some of the stalks too)

1 tsp celery seeds

1 cup super-steeped green tea (above), cooled

2 tsp agave syrup

1 pinch sea salt

Ice (optional)

1 tsp freshly squeezed lemon juice

Cold seltzer, to top

Celery stalk, to garnish

01 **Super-Steeped Green Tea:** Place the tea bags in the hot water and let steep for 15 minutes. Remove the tea bags and let cool.

02 **Cocktail:** Place the celery tops, celery seeds, super-steeped green tea, agave syrup and salt in a blender and blend for 1 minute.

03 Strain through a fine-mesh strainer or nut milk bag into a glass (if using ice, add it now). Add the lemon juice and top with cold seltzer. Gently swirl to combine. Garnish with a celery stalk and serve.

COCOAMOCO SELTZER

MAKES 1

NOTE
Be prepared to fall in
love with this recipe!
It's one of my faves.

Have you ever heard of chocolate egg cream? It's one of those old-fashioned things that sounds odd but is actually pretty good (and nostalgic). Oddly, egg cream has no egg or heavy cream in it whatsoever; it's just chocolate syrup, seltzer and milk. For this recipe, I swap the milk for a non-dairy option and add a touch of coffee to match the uplifting mood.

¼ cup cold non-dairy coffee creamer
  (my favorite is coconut creamer)
1 tbsp unsweetened cocoa powder
2 tsp instant coffee
1 tbsp maple syrup
½ tsp vanilla extract
Cold seltzer
Dark chocolate shavings, to top

01 Place the non-dairy coffee creamer, cocoa powder, instant coffee, maple syrup and vanilla in a tall glass and froth until combined (use one of those small frothers for the best results, but if you don't have one, use a fork and whisk vigorously). While frothing, slowly add the seltzer to fill the glass, being careful that it doesn't overflow.

02 Shave some dark chocolate on top and serve.

GREEN COCONUTS

MAKES 1

Have you ever had a fresh young coconut straight from the palm tree? It's insane. The coconut flavor comes through so differently than it does when it's mature or dried. Young coconut has a creamier texture and an almost milky-coconut taste (less nutty than its dried counterpart). I wanted to bring the essence of that fresh coconut taste into a drink. I mix it with green tea and coconut water to make it extra hydrating and uplifting.

1 cup coconut water

2 drops coconut extract (more if you like an intense coconut flavor)

½ cup cold green tea

1 tbsp freshly squeezed lemon juice

1 tbsp simple syrup (see p. 12)

1 dash Angostura or aromatic bitters

Ice

1 piece fresh young coconut meat or 1 piece dried coconut, to garnish

01 Stir the coconut water and extract, green tea, lemon juice, simple syrup and bitters in a mixing glass with ice.

02 Strain into a highball glass filled with ice. Garnish with coconut and enjoy.

WALNUT CHAI DOS LECHES

MAKES 1

What happens when you combine chai-like ingredients and a tres leches cake? This recipe! (Minus one of the leches ☺.) There is a sweet, caffeinated punch to this drink, almost like that of a liquid dessert, which calls for a slow, intentional sip. This recipe gives White Russian cocktail vibes but makes it millennial.

1 cup oat milk, or regular if you like

1 tbsp vegan condensed milk, or regular if you like

1 bag black tea

1 tsp ground cinnamon, plus more to finish

¼ tsp ground cloves

Ice, to serve (optional)

2 dashes walnut bitters

01 Place milks, tea bag, cinnamon and cloves in a small saucepan over medium-low heat. Simmer for 10 minutes, then remove from heat. Cool, then strain.

02 Pour the spiced milk into a glass, add ice if you wish (or serve at room temp) and finish with walnut bitters and a pinch of cinnamon.

FLAMING MARY

I'm pretty sure you are quite familiar with the Bloody Mary cocktail, an oldie but goodie. My mother loves a good Bloody Mary (extra spicy, of course), and the sight of one immediately transports me into childhood memories of relaxing at home on a weekend with my parents. I made this version for her; it has zero alcohol but is loaded with flavor and extra spice.

NOTE
Adjust the amount of chipotle peppers in adobo sauce for the spice level of your liking.

3 very ripe garden, Roma or on-the-vine tomatoes

1 tsp miso paste

1 tsp apple cider vinegar

¼ tsp celery salt

1 pinch hot pepper flakes

Zest and juice of 1 lemon

1 tsp freshly ground black pepper

1 tsp agave syrup

½ tsp chipotle peppers in adobo sauce

1 pinch salt, to top

Olives, to garnish

Ice, to serve (optional)

01   Place the tomatoes, miso, vinegar, celery salt, pepper flakes, lemon zest and juice, black pepper, agave syrup and chipotle peppers in adobo sauce in a blender. Blend until smooth, about 2 minutes.

02   Strain through a fine-mesh strainer into a glass, using a spoon to press the pulp into the strainer to extract every bit of liquid. Top with a pinch of salt, garnish with olives and serve at room temp or with ice.

Cele-
brate

86 .... OH MY GLÖGG

88 .... GINGER GLAM

91 .... APASIONADO

92 .... FOUNTAIN OF BEAUTY

95 .... GRANNY'S FAVE

96 .... SMOOTH WATERMELON

98 .... PEAR CINNAMON HEARTS

98 .... KARAT GOLD

99 .... POMEGRANATE SOUR

102 .... LA FLOR

105 .... MANGO TANGO

106 .... LYCHEE LOCA

109 .... PINEAPPLE JASMINE CUP

110 .... A SHOT OF JOY

112 .... THE GLOW

Citrus
Floral
Fruit-Forward

SETTING THE MOOD

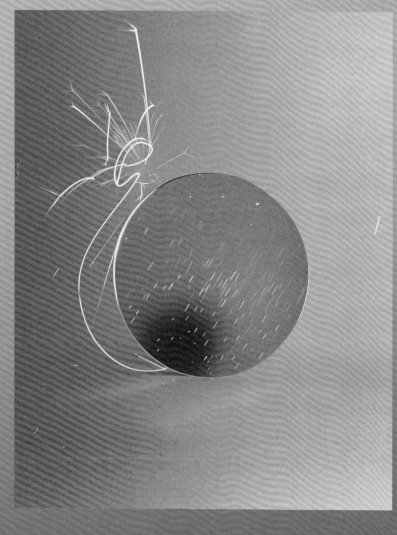

TO CELEBRATE

This mood is all about happiness, excitement and joy to celebrate with yourself or with others. Job promotions, birthday parties and personal milestones—these and more are all part of it.

SPACE

Celebration, whether it's solo or with company, is all about high energy and effervescence. Think of the bubbles in a drink, how they fizz and pop with excitement. You want this same feeling for your space of celebration. Now, celebrations don't happen every day (though you are totally allowed to do this), so unlike a chilling nook to relax, which is probably more of a permanent fixture in your routine, a celebratory space can be temporary.

To find the perfect spot, think of a place with high energy, something that feels open and inviting. Think of your dining or kitchen table, the floor in your living room, a garden or your balcony. Since this is a temporary space, you can make room for it whenever you need to and move a few things around so they're not in the way. My favorite space for celebration is my dining room table, since it's quite close to the kitchen. I usually celebrate with friends, and this spot allows me to entertain with ease. Even if I were to celebrate on my own, this spot faces my window, so it feels open and joyful.

OBJECTS

Sparkle, bright colors and interesting shapes all help create a celebratory mood. Think of dressing up for a party, when you add interest to your outfit with layers like earrings, necklaces or maybe a big bow. Similarly, trays, swizzle sticks, straws, garnishes and other layers add interest to a party. The goal here is to make it feel a little extra special. It's a celebration! You don't have to go overboard; simple details do the trick. Oversized or tall glassware and serving bowls deliver high impact and allow guests to interact.

For materials, think of mouth-blown glassware, metal or anything with a high gloss that reflects light and sparkles. My favorite vessel for celebration is a faceted coupe. It makes any drink look fancy! And the facets in the glass reflect the light onto my table and hand, making everything feel extra special.

ATMOSPHERE

To set the mood to celebrate, you'll need a few things to tie it all together. Let's start with lighting. You can set the scene to be quite dark, like a cool, underground party, and use only a few sources of light. Perhaps you can even use one of those color-changing light bulbs and set it to something bright and fun. (A bright orange light in a corner? Very groovy!) If you like something a bit brighter, just make sure no sources of light are directly in front of people, and avoid harsh overhead lighting.

Celebrations also need a fun playlist. Plan ahead and find a few playlists that will set the tone. A party is like a movie; it starts slow as it introduces the characters, then goes into high gear to bring the story to life, and ends with a big climax. Do the same for your playlist; start with music that's nice and slow, then kick it up so that everyone gets into the groove, and end with something chill or "oldies" that everyone loves (this is also a very polite way of telling people "Time to go home!").

Lastly, scent! Can you use scent to bring about the best mood to celebrate? Absolutely. Try anything that feels bubbly, fresh and like a burst of energy: fruity, spicy and floral scents will do the trick. If you don't want to have a candle burning during the celebration, you can spray a scent before people arrive (or when you're about to celebrate with yourself). You can also use the drink itself as the scent. My favorite type of dual-use drink and scent is a big bowl of punch. You can smell the fruit in it, it's bubbly and full of color and it brings people together.

OH MY GLÖGG

SERVES 4

During one of my trips to the Nordics, I was visiting a friend for the holidays when I tried glögg for the first time. Glögg is the Nordic version of a mulled wine—very similar, in fact. I really liked the taste of it, but the combination of sugar and alcohol from the red wine would trigger some serious regrets the next day, so I've created this non-alcoholic version. I love the feeling this punch cocktail brings to a gathering. It's celebratory, full of flavor and quite easy to make.

NOTE
This recipe is served chilled, but you can skip the ice and serve it hot during colder months.

3 cups non-alcoholic red wine

2 cups pomegranate juice

1 cup freshly squeezed orange juice, strained (no pulp)

Peel of 1 lime

1 tbsp brown sugar

5 cloves

2 tsp vanilla extract

5 cinnamon sticks

2 tbsp orange bitters

Ice

Lemon slices, to garnish

01 Place the non-alcoholic red wine, pomegranate juice, orange juice, lime peel, sugar, cloves, vanilla, cinnamon sticks and bitters in a saucepan over low heat and simmer for 15 minutes. Remove from heat and let cool to room temperature. Strain through a fine-mesh strainer into a clean container and discard all the spices.

02 Fill a jug with ice, add the lemon slices and pour in the cooled mixture. Serve.

GINGER GLAM

MAKES 1

Ginger beer and fresh ginger. This feels like a mule, but it's more than that. When served, this drink has lovely golden tones that make it look like a cup worthy of a celebration. There's glam in every drop, so sip carefully and don't let it get to your head.

½ cup unsweetened iced tea
1 tsp freshly grated ginger
1 tbsp freshly squeezed lemon juice
½ tsp Angostura or aromatic bitters
Ginger beer, to top

01 Combine the iced tea, ginger, lemon juice and bitters in a glass, and swirl with a bar spoon. Let sit for 10 minutes to infuse.

02 Strain into a serving glass of your choice. Top with ginger beer and serve.

APASIONADO

Passion fruit is one of those ingredients that feels quite bougie. If you look at old paintings, things like passion fruit are being eaten by gods or royalty. Thankfully, times have changed and we can all enjoy passion fruit here and there. I really like this cocktail for spring and summer celebrations because it feels like a royal treat. Passion fruit has lots of floral notes so it's almost like a dual celebration—one that includes a drink and a bouquet of flowers.

¼ cup passion fruit puree

¼ cup freshly squeezed orange juice

1½ tbsp freshly squeezed lemon juice

Zest of ½ lemon

½ tsp vanilla paste

3 tbsp non-alcoholic gin (see p. 12)

2 dashes aromatic bitters

½ to 1 cup ice (depending on the slushy consistency you like)

01 Place all ingredients in a blender and blend until slushy. Pour into a coupe glass and serve.

FOUNTAIN OF BEAUTY

SERVES 4

One of my best friends grew up in Munich, where they enjoy drinking Hugo cocktails in the summer. A Hugo is made with prosecco, elderflower syrup and sparkling water. For this version, I removed the alcohol and added a touch of spice with flavored distilled water (found in brands like Seedlip). You can also make your own by simply boiling a few spices in water. The final touch of edible flowers as a garnish makes this drink feel like an oasis—hence the name.

½ cup white or champagne grapes, frozen

½ cup spiced distilled water (Seedlip or similar), cold

3 tbsp elderflower syrup

1 tbsp verjus (add more if you like tartness)

1 bottle non-alcoholic dry prosecco, cold

Edible flowers, to garnish

01 Place the grapes, distilled water, elderflower syrup and verjus in a big serving bowl or jug pour in the non-alcoholic prosecco and very gently stir to combine. Garnish with edible flowers and serve.

GRANNY'S FAVE

SERVES 4

Granny Smith apples are an oldie but a goodie! I say "oldie" because this type of apple seemed to be all the rage in recipes back in the 90s and early 2000s. Since I am a millennial who seeks every opportunity to do a good 90s revival, you bet I want to bring these apples back.

This drink packs a little kick by way of jalapeño, and you can add as much or as little as you need to bring the heat to the party. This drink is perfect when you are getting ready to go out with a bunch of friends and you need something that will get everyone in the mood to revive those 90s dance moves.

Granny's Fave Base
4 Granny Smith apples

1 cup water

Zest and juice of 1 lemon

¼ cup super-steeped green tea (see p. 61), cooled

1 tsp vanilla extract

2 tbsp brown sugar

½ tsp salt

½ jalapeño

1 pinch salt

Cocktail
½ cup Granny's fave base (above)

1 tsp simple syrup (see p. 12)

2 dashes aromatic bitters

Ice

1 apple coin (cut with a melon baller), to garnish

01   **Granny's Fave Base:** Core the Granny Smith apples and cut into chunks. Place the chunks in a blender with all the other ingredients. Blend on high until smooth, about 2 minutes. Strain the liquid through a fine-mesh strainer or nut milk bag into a clean airtight container. This will keep in the fridge for up to 1 week.

02   **Cocktail:** Place the Granny's fave base, simple syrup and aromatic bitters into a shaker with ice. Shake for 1 to 2 minutes, until the shaker is frosty.

03   Strain into a chilled coupe-style glass. Thread the apple coin onto a pick to garnish, and serve.

SMOOTH WATERMELON

MAKES 1

This drink is silky and refreshing, and before you know it, it'll become one of your favorites. Just like a summer fling! Music is a big influence for my recipe inspiration. If you haven't guessed, this drink came to be thanks to Sade's famous song "Smooth Operator." I wanted to translate the feeling, vibes and easiness of this song into a delicious drink. Watermelon, rich coconut cream and a few other ingredients made it all come together. Be warned: this drink will 100% try to put the moves on you.

1 cup watermelon chunks

¼ cup aloe juice

2 tbsp canned coconut cream

2 tbsp freshly squeezed lime juice

1 pinch salt

Ice, to serve

Watermelon slice or fresh mint, to garnish (optional)

01 Place watermelon, aloe juice, coconut cream, lime juice and salt in a blender and blend until smooth, about 1 minute.

02 Pour into a glass with ice. Garnish with watermelon or mint and serve.

1

PEAR CINNAMON HEARTS

MAKES 1

This drink was created for an intimate celebration (for one or two). Cinnamon has a wonderful ability to heat up the body and mind, and pear has a soft, subtle taste that's very sensual. This is all about getting you in the mood, catch my drift? Wink, wink.

¼ cup pear nectar

¼ cup super-steeped chamomile tea (see p. 127), cooled

1 tbsp freshly squeezed lemon juice

1 tsp vanilla extract

½ tsp cinnamon extract

½ tsp ground cinnamon

¼ tsp cocktail foamer (see p. 11)

Ice

Pear slice, to garnish

01 Place the pear nectar, chamomile tea, lemon juice, vanilla, cinnamon extract, ground cinnamon and cocktail foamer in a shaker. Dry shake for about 1 minute. Add ice and shake again until the shaker gets frosty.

02 Strain into a nice fancy glass and garnish with a pear slice.

2

KARAT GOLD

MAKES 1

This drink is one of the brunchiest things you'll ever try! Part health elixir, part fragrant cocktail, this is going to be a team favorite in no time. The liquid gold comes from a mix of fresh carrots (See what I did there? *Karat* gold! ☺), citrus syrup and coconut water. There's a little fizz in there, plus a dash of bitters to round it all up.

½ cup carrot juice (freshly made is best, but you do you)

¼ cup coconut water

1½ tsp yuzu syrup (see note)

Ice

1 dash cardamom bitters or aromatic bitters

Tonic water, to top

Lime leaf, to garnish (optional)

01 In a tall glass, combine the carrot juice, coconut water and yuzu syrup. Stir well until the syrup dissolves. Fill the glass with ice, add a dash of bitters and top with tonic water. Garnish with a lime leaf.

NOTE
This drink will make any celebration come to life, guaranteed! You can purchase yuzu syrup online, in specialty liquor or bartender shops or in some Japanese markets. If you can't find yuzu syrup, substitute with 1 tsp agave syrup and 1 tsp freshly squeezed lemon juice.

3

POMEGRANATE SOUR

MAKES 1

Pomegranate is the star of this drink. The natural tartness of pomegranate juice brings forth lots of glorious fruity tannins, and I added a touch of cinnamon vanilla syrup to echo a classic "rum" tasting note. The garnish for this drink is a maraschino cherry, but feel free to instead use a nice chunk of fresh pomegranate, if in season. It'll look quite juicy, decadent and celebratory.

Cinnamon Vanilla Syrup

1 cup water

½ cup granulated sugar

5 cinnamon sticks

½ vanilla bean, split in half

Cocktail

½ cup pomegranate juice

2 tbsp freshly squeezed lemon juice

1 tbsp orgeat syrup

½ tbsp cinnamon vanilla syrup (above)

½ tsp aromatic or orange bitters

¼ tsp cocktail foamer (see p. 11)

Ice

1 maraschino cherry, to garnish

01 **Cinnamon Vanilla Syrup:** Place all ingredients in a small saucepan over medium heat. Bring to a boil, then reduce the heat to low and simmer until reduced by half. Let cool, then transfer to a clean glass jar to store (no need to strain). This syrup will keep in the fridge for about 1 week.

02 **Cocktail:** Place the pomegranate juice, lemon juice, orgeat syrup, cinnamon vanilla syrup, bitters and cocktail foamer in a shaker and dry shake for about 30 seconds. Add ice to the shaker and shake again for a minute or two until the shaker turns frosty.

03 Strain into a chilled glass and garnish with a maraschino cherry.

1-PEAR CINNAMON HEARTS

2-KARAT GOLD

3-POMEGRANATE SOUR

LA FLOR

I am channeling some serious Selena Quintanilla flor vibes into this recipe. This punch drink is so fun to make for a gathering, and it gets extra points for looking party-ready with lots of floral ice cubes. In Mexico we drink a lot of agua de sabor, which in English most people call "agua fresca." It's all the same: a base of tea or fruit with one or two complementary ingredients to bring it all together. The inspiration for this drink comes from a winter holiday punch recipe my mom makes, so it's been family-tested for several generations.

NOTE
Feel free to add more fruit like strawberries, blueberries or anything else that would make this celebration drink extra colorful.

2 cups water

2 cups non-alcoholic sparkling dry apple cider, plus more to finish

¼ cup freshly squeezed lemon juice

1 orange, quartered

½ cup pineapple chunks (preferably fresh, but frozen work too)

¼ cup dried hibiscus flowers

10 juniper berries

5 cloves

1 sprig fresh tarragon

1 tsp vanilla extract

¼ cup piloncillo, raw cane sugar or brown sugar

Floral ice, to serve (freeze some edible flowers in water in ice cube trays)

01   Place the water, cider, lemon juice, orange quarters, pineapple, hibiscus flowers, juniper berries, cloves, tarragon, vanilla and piloncillo in a large pot. Bring to a simmer over medium-low heat. Simmer for 10 minutes, then remove from heat and let cool. Strain the contents into a clean container and refrigerate for at least 2 hours before serving.

02   To serve, pour the punch into a punch bowl or jug and add the floral ice cubes. Scoop into coupe glasses and add a splash of sparkling apple cider to each glass to finish.

MANGO TANGO

MAKES 1

Have you ever eaten a super ripe mango over a sink? If you haven't, my friend, you haven't lived a full life yet. Mangoes that are in season are an addiction of mine. There's nothing like it! Sweet, creamy, floral, fruity flesh. Sounds X-rated, but that's the magic of a ripe mango. Since mangoes are not always in season, having one always feels like a special occasion, so I needed to include a drink loaded with fresh mango for a moment of celebration. (If you're craving this cocktail but you can't find ripe mangoes in season, use frozen.)

NOTE
This recipe needs an overnight infusion, so plan ahead.

Mango Tango Infusion
¼ cup packed fresh chamomile or 5 bags chamomile tea

½ English cucumber, halved, seeded and cut into chunks

10 juniper berries, crushed

5 pods cardamom, crushed

4 bags jasmine tea

2 cups water

Peel of 1 lemon

Peel of 1 lime

Cocktail
¼ cup fresh ripe or thawed frozen mango chunks

1 pinch salt

2 tbsp simple syrup (see p. 12)

1 tbsp freshly squeezed lemon juice

⅓ cup mango tango infusion (above)

Crushed ice

1 mango spear, to garnish

1 lemon wedge, to garnish

01 **Mango Tango Infusion:** Place all ingredients in a small pot and bring to a simmer over low heat. Remove from heat and let cool. Transfer to a clean glass jar and leave in the fridge overnight (do not strain; leave everything in to infuse). The next day, strain through a fine-mesh strainer into a clean container. This infusion keeps in the fridge for about 1 week.

02 **Cocktail:** In an old-fashioned-style glass, muddle the mango chunks, salt, syrup and lemon juice. Add the mango tango infusion and top with crushed ice. Gently stir to combine. Garnish with a mango spear and lemon wedge.

LYCHEE LOCA

I love, l-o-v-e, lychee. It's such a unique-tasting fruit that people either love it or hate it. This drink uses lychee syrup, which is a bit milder than the fresh fruit. I combined it with a bit of pineapple juice and a touch of citrus to make it sing. Honestly, I had this drink quite a few times (basically until I finished the can of lychee) after I tested it. It's delicious and oh so refreshing.

¼ cup lychee syrup (from a can of lychees in syrup)

⅓ cup pineapple juice

1 tbsp freshly squeezed lime juice

2 tbsp non-alcoholic gin or similar non-alcoholic spirit

Ice

1 small bouquet fresh mint, to garnish

1 small piece fresh lychee, to garnish (optional)

01　Place the lychee syrup, pineapple juice, lime juice and non-alcoholic gin in a tall glass filled with ice. Gently swirl with a bar spoon to combine. Garnish with mint and fresh lychee.

PINEAPPLE JASMINE CUP

MAKES 1

Jasmine has one of the strongest floral notes out there, which works to our advantage when making a drink, since we don't have to use a ton of it. This drink is giving me main-character vibes.

Super-Steeped Jasmine Tea
4 bags or 1 tbsp loose-leaf jasmine tea
½ cup hot water

Cocktail
½ cup pineapple juice
¼ cup super-steeped jasmine tea (above), cooled
1 tbsp orgeat syrup
1 tbsp freshly squeezed lime juice
¼ tsp cocktail foamer (see p. 11)
Ice
2 dashes cardamom bitters or aromatic bitters

01 **Super-Steeped Jasmine Tea:** Place the tea bags or loose-leaf tea in the hot water and let steep for at least 15 minutes. Remove the tea bags (or strain if needed) and let cool.

02 **Cocktail:** Place the pineapple juice, jasmine tea, orgeat, lime juice, and cocktail foamer in a shaker and dry shake for 1 minute. Add the ice and shake until frosty. Strain into a coupe or similar glass, add the bitters and serve.

A SHOT OF JOY

SERVES 4

This recipe feels like a grown-up, feel-good, healthy-ish version of doing shots at the club. The best part is, you can do these from the comfort of your own home. You can even make them a little extra bougie by using glassware with personality, like vintage liqueur glasses or small espresso cups. I highly recommend these shots for weekend gatherings and early-day celebrations.

Super-Steeped Jasmine Tea

3 bags or 1 tbsp loose-leaf jasmine tea

1 cup hot water

Cocktail

½ ripe cantaloupe, peeled, seeded and cut into chunks

1 cup super-steeped jasmine tea (above), cooled

1 tsp orange blossom water

½-inch knob fresh ginger

Zest and juice of 2 lemons

1 tsp umeboshi paste

01 **Super-Steeped Jasmine Tea:** Place the tea bags or loose-leaf tea in the hot water and let steep for 15 minutes. Remove the tea bags (or strain if needed) and let cool.

02 **Cocktail:** Place all ingredients in a blender and blend on high for 2 to 3 minutes, until smooth. Strain through a fine-mesh strainer or nut milk bag. Refrigerate for at least 1 hour before serving. Serve in chilled shot glasses.

THE GLOW

This is like a supercharged, zero-proof mimosa, but even tastier. The glow juice is packed with oranges, turmeric and coconut water. When you combine all of that with sparkling non-alcoholic prosecco, you get an instant crowd-pleaser. I love that this drink is also super hydrating and naturally sweet from the fresh fruit.

NOTE
Play with the ratio of glow juice and bubbles to your liking. As we say in Mexico, some people like it "pintada" (just a touch of juice), and there's nothing wrong with that. ☺

Glow Juice
1 cup freshly squeezed satsuma mandarin, sumo or regular orange juice

½ lemon, peeled and seeded

½ cup coconut water

1 tsp ground turmeric

1 tsp orange blossom water (less if you don't like it too floral)

1 pinch salt

Per Cocktail
2 tbsp glow juice (above), cold

Non-alcoholic prosecco, cold

Orange peel, to garnish

01 **Glow Juice:** Place all ingredients in a blender and blend on high for 1 to 2 minutes, until smooth. Strain a few times through a fine-mesh strainer or nut milk bag into a clean container. This juice will keep in the fridge for about 3 days.

02 **Cocktail:** Pour the glow juice (adjust amount to your liking) into a champagne glass and gently top with cold non-alcoholic prosecco. Garnish with an orange peel and serve.

Ex-plore

118........GRAPE STALLION

121........PLUM BLOSSOM SHRUB

122........GO BANANAS

124........SAGE AWAY

127........RHUBARBARA

128........TEPACHE PUNCH

130........THE EVERGREEN

131........PURPLE CLOUDS

131........WOODY BOOCH

135........UMAMILADA

136........PICKLED COOLER

138........NUTTYRATO

141........GOCHU SODA

143........TINGLY CUKES

144........OIL PAINTING

Funky Fermented Oddball

SETTING THE MOOD TO

EXPLORE

This mood is all about the feel that comes with newness. It's a little exciting, but also different and out of your comfort zone. It's like a mini adventure of your own!

SPACE

Exploration is all about trying, searching, even traveling. To set this mood, create a space that is conducive to discovery, like a lab. You can set up a drink cart or even a small space in your kitchen to mix up new concoctions. You can also have a satellite space, like a friend's house, where you meet to explore. This space can be temporary or permanent, it all depends on your routine. Some people love to experiment and constantly try new things, so a permanent space makes more sense, while others get in the mood to explore only once in a while.

To get into the flow of experimentation, creation and discovery, it's best to have an area with all of your tools handy. My favorite space for exploring is my kitchen counter. I have added extra space with a cart that holds all my tools, books and special glassware.

OBJECTS

Organization is your best friend here: think shelves, nicely stacked vessels, all sorts of spoons and labels for exotic ingredients. When inspiration strikes, you want to be ready. Just like when you're cooking, you want to have your most-used utensils nearby and organized—there's nothing more annoying than constantly rattling through drawers trying to find something.

This is where high-end design items can come out to play. Some of these items are not very comfortable for everyday use, but they are totally fine to get you excited about exploring. Specialty tools, interesting materials and one-of-a-kinds should be part of this. Think metals that age well (chrome, bronze, stainless steel), wood and heavy glass—things that feel good in the hand and will develop a patina as you wear them out. In terms of glassware, anything that's design-forward and unique is perfect. Feel free to step away from the classics; try using a nice tea bowl instead of a drink glass. One of my favorite pieces for when I'm in the mood to explore is a handmade glass with a chubby, squiggly handle. It's so fun! And it makes my funky drink look like a chic lab experiment.

ATMOSPHERE

You probably want a well-lit space to create and explore. Since you're in a discovery mood, you want to be able to see what you're making. If the area you chose doesn't have much light, add a lamp nearby (I recommend a slightly warm bright bulb). Setting a schedule also helps; maybe your space gets the best light in the evenings, so plan ahead to explore during this time.

Music conducive to exploring is crucial. You want something vibey and slightly chill, with a groove. Play something that helps you move but is not too energetic (you're creating and exploring, not partying). Background-type music is great for this.

To tie it all together, let's add a scent. You would think that for this kind of mood you would like something funky and intricate, but this could have the opposite effect and hijack your attention. You want to focus on your drink making, not on the scent itself. A good neutral base is best for exploring: think of clean linens, one-note scents like lemongrass or even a subtle natural vanilla (not the super-strong and artificial kind). My favorite scent for exploring comes from freshly washed linen cloths that I use to wipe my glassware. It puts me right in the mood to be creative and try something new.

GRAPE STALLION

MAKES 1

This drink feels like a mini vacation in Italy, with all its deliciously bitter drinks, sodas and—you guessed it—Italian stallions! It's like a steamy novel in the making. If you are a fan of deeply herbaceous, bitter drinks, then this is for you.

NOTE
This recipe has a few components that need to be made in advance, so—just like planning a good vacation—you need to plan accordingly.

Grape Stallion Base
3 bags Earl Grey tea
¼ cup water
3 cups grape juice
Peel of ½ pomelo or grapefruit
5 juniper berries
1 pinch salt

Quick Pickle Grapes
½ cup water
¼ cup port vinegar or red wine vinegar
3 tbsp granulated sugar
1 tsp sea salt
10 grapes

Cocktail
⅓ cup grape stallion base (above)
3 tsp freshly squeezed lemon juice
Handful of ice
Quick pickle grapes (above), to garnish

01 **Grape Stallion Base:** Place all ingredients in a small pot and simmer over low heat for 15 minutes. Let cool for another 20 minutes or so, then strain and use. Save any leftover base for another drink; it will keep in the fridge for up to 1 week.

02 **Quick Pickle Grapes:** Place water, vinegar, sugar and salt in a small pot. Bring to a simmer over medium heat and simmer until the sugar dissolves, a couple of minutes. Remove from heat and let cool. Add the grapes and let them sit in the mixture for at least 30 minutes. Strain though a fine-mesh strainer into a clean airtight container. The pickled grapes will keep in the fridge for up to 3 days.

03 **Cocktail:** Place the grape stallion base, lemon juice and ice in a shaker. Shake until frosty, about 30 seconds.

04 Strain into a clean coupe or martini glass. Garnish with a grape and serve.

PLUM BLOSSOM SHRUB

MAKES 1

I recently discovered that there is a tea made out of the blossoms of the plum tree. The taste of it totally blew my mind. It has this mellow, sweet amaretto note with just a touch of bitterness. I tried it in different ways—hot, room temp and iced—and each version yields such a different taste! For this recipe we are turning the blossoms into a drink that is part shrub, part aperitivo.

NOTE
You can find plum blossom tea in specialty tea stores or online.

Super-Steeped Plum Blossom Tea
2 tbsp plum blossom tea leaves
½ cup hot water

Cocktail
Ice
⅓ cup apple cider, cold
¼ cup super-steeped plum blossom tea (above), cold
1 tsp port vinegar or sherry vinegar
2 dashes Angostura or aromatic bitters
Splash of sparkling water (optional)
Fresh plum slice, to garnish

01 **Super-Steeped Plum Blossom Tea:** Place the tea in the hot water and let steep for at least 15 minutes. Let cool, then strain. Keep leftover tea for another cocktail; it will keep in the fridge for up to 1 week.

02 **Cocktail:** In a glass with ice, combine the apple cider, super-steeped plum blossom tea, vinegar and bitters and stir to combine.

03 Strain into a cute glass and add a splash of sparkling water. Garnish with a plum slice and serve.

GO BANANAS

MAKES 1

Banana is something you don't often see in a non-alcoholic cocktail. I think it's tricky to use without the whole thing turning into a smoothie. I did some digging, though, and I found a way to incorporate the natural taste of bananas without using artificial flavoring (and without turning it into a smoothie). The result is a quasi mix of banana and floral tea notes. It's definitely a new flavor to discover.

NOTE
This recipe needs the syrup to macerate for 24 hours, so plan ahead. By the way, malt tea has a bit of a whiskey, woody aftertaste. I found it at my local specialty tea shop, but you can also order it online.

Banana Orgeat Syrup

2 cups water

1 cup granulated sugar

¼ cup orgeat syrup

3 banana peels (wash the skin before peeling the bananas, not after)

1 large piece orange peel

Super-Steeped Malt Tea

2 bags or 1 tbsp loose-leaf malt tea

½ cup hot water

Cocktail

Ice

½ cup super-steeped malt tea (above)

2 tbsp banana orgeat syrup (above)

2 dashes pineapple bitters

1 dash vanilla bitters or aromatic bitters

01 **Banana Orgeat Syrup:** Place the water, sugar and orgeat in a clean container and stir to dissolve. Add the banana and orange peels, gently mash with a wooden spoon, then cover and place in the fridge for 24 hours. The next day, strain into a clean airtight container. It'll keep in the fridge for about 1 week.

02 **Super-Steeped Malt Tea:** Place the tea bags or loose-leaf tea in the hot water and let steep for at least 15 minutes. Remove the tea bags (or strain if needed) and let cool.

03 **Cocktail:** In a mixing glass with ice, combine the malt tea, banana orgeat syrup and bitters and stir until frosty. Strain and serve in a fun glass.

SAGE AWAY

MAKES 1

This drink has a personal story behind it. The very first CD my parents bought was Enya's eponymous album, and it was a hit around the house. When Enya came out with her second album, *Watermark*, the song "Orinoco Flow" was an immediate family anthem. The "sail away" chorus was being whistled day in and day out. I remember the soothing feeling of discovering this new-to-me kind of music (indie, pop, Celtic). As young as I was, I already knew this kind of music made for a moment of contemplation.

While trying to come up with recipes for this chapter, "Orinoco Flow" made its way into my playlist, and as I whistled the main chorus, "sage away" came to my mind. Aha! A drink to discover and contemplate? With deep notes of sage as the base? It's perfect! So here it is, a concoction born out of childhood contemplation.

NOTE
I seriously hope you play Enya while you enjoy this drink.

Sage Infusion
10 fresh sage leaves
5 juniper berries
1 small piece lemon peel
1 pod cardamom, smashed
3 black peppercorns
1 bag green tea
1 cup water
2 tbsp agave syrup

Cocktail
⅓ cup sage infusion (above)
1 large ice cube
5 dashes pineapple bitters or aromatic bitters
1 fresh sage leaf, to garnish

01 **Sage Infusion:** Place all ingredients in a small pot over low heat, and simmer for 15 minutes. Remove from heat and let cool, then place in a clean glass jar in the fridge for at least 1 hour (longer is better). This will keep in the fridge for up to 3 days.

02 **Cocktail:** Place the sage infusion in a mixing glass with an ice cube. Swirl until the glass gets frosty.

03 Strain the contents into a coupe, add the pineapple bitters, garnish with a fresh sage leaf and serve.

RHUBARBARA

MAKES 1

The name of this cocktail is a mix of its key ingredients and the Mexican Spanish expression "que Barbara!"—which is similar to "omg!" and can be used when pleasantly surprised with something. This combination of rhubarb, strawberry and tonic water is just that: a very pleasant surprise that tastes like a creamsicle! It's kinda wild and unexpected, and an absolute joy to sip on a hot day.

Super-Steeped Chamomile Tea

3 bags chamomile tea

1 cup hot water

Cocktail

1½ stalks fresh rhubarb, washed and trimmed, or
  ¼ cup frozen rhubarb chunks, plus more if you like
  it extra tart

5 strawberries, hulled and sliced

1 large piece orange peel

1 tbsp agave syrup

1 cup super-steeped chamomile tea, cooled

½ tsp vanilla extract

Ice

Tonic water, to top

Strawberry slice, to garnish

01 **Super-Steeped Chamomile Tea:** Place the tea bags in the hot water and let steep for 15 minutes. Remove the tea bags and let cool.

02 Place the rhubarb, strawberries, orange peel, agave syrup, chamomile tea and vanilla in a small saucepan over low heat and simmer for 10 minutes. Remove from heat, mash with a fork or a wooden spoon and let cool. Strain into a clean glass jar, making sure to squeeze the pulp to get as much of the concentrate out as possible.

03 Pour the concentrate into a tall glass filled with ice, then top with tonic water. Garnish with a strawberry slice and serve.

TEPACHE PUNCH

SERVES 4

Tepache is a funky little drink that's super easy to make. It's usually made out of fermented pineapple rinds and sugar—pretty straightforward!—but that takes a little time. For this version, I kinda skipped the days-on-end fermentation of the pineapple, and instead I roasted it and let it sit overnight, which brings out the best tasting notes in a short time. I added a few extra ingredients that aren't classic of tepache but that totally complement the flavors and make it a punch.

NOTE
This recipe has to sit overnight, so plan accordingly. This punch can be enjoyed cold or at room temp with no ice.

Tepache Punch Base

1 overripe pineapple (when it starts to smell extra sweet and ferment-y, it's good to use)

1 pinch sea salt

1 tsp vanilla extract

½ cup piloncillo or ¼ cup packed brown sugar

5 cinnamon sticks

3 cloves

3 black peppercorns

½ cup freshly squeezed orange juice

3 cups water

Per Serving

Ice (optional)

¼ cup tepache punch base (above), or more if you like it intense

Cold seltzer, to top

1 dash orange bitters or aromatic bitters

01   **Tepache Punch Base:** Preheat the oven to 400°F. Peel the pineapple, remove the core and cut into chunks. Place the pineapple chunks on a baking tray lined with parchment paper or aluminum foil. Bake for 25 minutes, or until the pineapple chunks are dark and roasted. Remove from the oven and let the pineapple cool.

02   Place the roasted pineapple chunks and all other ingredients in a blender, and blend on high for 1 minute. Transfer the blended pineapple mixture to a clean glass jar and cover with a clean towel or mesh. Leave on your countertop overnight. The next day, cover with a lid and refrigerate. Your tepache punch base is now ready for use. It will keep in the fridge for up to 1 week.

03   **To Serve:** Fill a glass with ice (or serve at room temperature), add the tepache punch base, top with seltzer and add a dash of bitters.

1

THE EVERGREEN

MAKES 1

This drink is mega herbaceous and has quite the bite! It's very suitable for a night of exploring something new and tangy. I took the base inspiration from Brazilian lemonade, which uses whole limes, peel and all. Then there's the added ingredient of chlorophyll, which makes this drink intensely green, fresh and vibrant. It's seriously a breath of fresh air!

½ lime, peel left on

1 cup water

1 sprig fresh mint

½ tbsp liquid chlorophyll
   (I recommend the minty kind)

1 tbsp agave syrup

Handful of ice

Lime square, to garnish

01   Place the lime, water, mint, chlorophyll, agave syrup and ice in a blender and blend for 30 seconds, until fully broken up. Let sit in the blender for 15 minutes for all the flavors to mingle.

02   Strain through a fine-mesh strainer into a martini-style glass or something fancy. Garnish with the lime square and serve.

NOTE
You can find liquid chlorophyll in most health-food stores and online. To make the lime square, cut a rectangular strip of lime peel, then trim off the ends to make a square.

2

PURPLE CLOUDS

MAKES 1

This drink is made with a yogurt-based beverage called Calpico. Combining this base with lavender and black currant syrup, you get this tangy, fruity, creamy drink that's kinda wild on the taste buds.

1 cup Calpico

2 tbsp black currant syrup (Ribena or similar)

1 tsp dried lavender

1 tsp vanilla extract

¼ cup ice cubes

Edible flower, to garnish

01   Place all ingredients in a blender and blend for about 1 minute, or until frothy. Pour into the glass of your liking, garnish with an edible flower and serve.

NOTE
Feel free to adjust the amount of lavender used in this recipe to match your taste.

3

WOODY BOOCH

MAKES 1

This drink may come with some daddy issues, but we are making it anyway. A few years ago, I had this streak where I would go to a famous hotel lounge here in Vancouver and order an old-fashioned cocktail. It was more about the experience than the drink itself; heavy leather seats, lots of wood and a faint scent of something smoky (no one was smoking, but you could almost smell tobacco). I wanted a drink with all those vibes: kinda sexy, kinda woody, but updated. After many attempts, the best combination was actually the most minimal: kombucha, bitters and orange. As they say, easy does it!

Ice

½ cup plain kombucha

1 tbsp freshly squeezed orange juice

1 tsp smoke and oak bitters or other smoky bitters

2 tsp brown sugar simple syrup (see p. 12)

1 twist lemon, to garnish (optional)

01   Fill a small glass with ice, then add the kombucha, orange juice, bitters and brown sugar simple syrup. Gently swirl with a bar spoon to combine. Garnish with a lemon twist and serve.

NOTE
Feel free to play with the ratio of smoke and oak bitters depending on how woody you like it.

RECIPES ON PG 130-131

UMAMILADA

I recommend serving
this with a side of
pickled veggies, olives
or seaweed.

We already did a version of the michelada in the Uplift chapter, but
I wanted to do a second version that has no spice but lots of umami
notes instead. Umami is an extra flavor that's richly, deeply savory—
certain mushrooms, miso paste and parmesan cheese all have deep
umami notes, which is why we all love them so much. This drink uses
mushroom broth, soy sauce and pickle brine, so get ready for the
umami trip of a lifetime.

Mushroom Broth

1 cup hot water

1 cube mushroom broth

Cocktail

Ice

½ cup tomato juice

1 tsp soy sauce or tamari, plus more if you
   like salty notes

¼ cup mushroom broth (above), cooled

1 tbsp pickle brine

1 tbsp freshly squeezed lime juice

1½ cups non-alcoholic beer

1 lemon wheel, to garnish

01 **Mushroom Broth:** In a small bowl, combine the hot water and broth
cube. Using a fork or small whisk, break up the cube and stir until fully
dissolved. Let the broth cool before using. You can keep the leftover
broth in the fridge for up to 1 week.

02 **Cocktail:** Fill a tall glass with ice. Add the tomato juice, soy sauce,
broth, pickle brine and lime juice. Top with the non-alcoholic beer and
very gently swirl to combine. Garnish with a lemon wheel and serve.

PICKLED COOLER

MAKES 1

Not gonna lie, this drink is intense. It has heat, brine and saltiness. It's meant to be served in small amounts with lots of ice, so it's more of a refresher. Pickled anything seems to be all the rage these days. I'm happy this trend has taken off and is sticking around. Personally, I love a good savory cocktail that will make me pay attention to the ingredients I'm tasting. I also love a good "Whoa! What's this?" moment. So if you are into all those things too, go ahead and make yourself a glass of this dirty pickled cooler.

Ice

3-inch piece cucumber peel

1 tsp Hungarian pepper brine or jalapeño pepper brine

1 tsp olive brine

1 tsp freshly squeezed lemon juice

⅓ cup non-alcoholic gin or spiced distilled water (Seedlip or similar)

1 pinch sea salt

Club soda, to top

01   Fill a tall glass with ice and wiggle the cucumber peel in between the ice. Add the pepper brine, olive brine, lemon juice, non-alcoholic gin and salt and gently swirl to combine. Top with club soda and serve.

NUTTYRATO

MAKES 1

Have you tried a shakerato? It's this coffee that you shake vigorously with ice until frothy. It's quite a tasty drink! For this version, I went a little extra with a few ingredients that add a layer of nutty flavors: toasted rice, hazelnut syrup and vanilla, my oh my. Don't know if you're ready for it.

Ice

½ cup cold brewed coffee

¼ cup brewed Korean brown rice tea or hojicha

1 tbsp hazelnut syrup

¼ tsp vanilla extract

Shaved toasted hazelnuts, to top (optional)

01 In a shaker with ice, combine the brewed coffee, brown rice tea, hazelnut syrup and vanilla. Shake until the shaker gets frosty, about a minute or two.

02 Strain into a small glass, top with shaved hazelnuts and serve.

GOCHU SODA

MAKES 1

I love a drink that takes your taste buds by surprise, especially the ones that have an expected combination of textures and flavors. So you bet your fancy coupes that I had to include some weird version of an aperitivo soda in this book. I remember tasting a version of a chamoy paloma in Mexico that captivated my palate. Chamoy and gochujang are kinda like cousins, except the latter is a fermented Korean chili paste. This drink is sweet, salty and a touch bitter. Not for the faint of heart.

NOTE
Adjust the amount of gochujang paste according to your spice tolerance.

¼ cup non-alcoholic aperitivo
  (like Ghia or Roots Divino)

1 tsp agave syrup

2 tsp freshly squeezed lemon juice

½ tsp gochujang paste

Ice

Grapefruit soda, to top

01 Place the non-alcoholic aperitivo, agave syrup, lemon juice and gochujang paste in a small bowl. Stir until all ingredients are combined.

02 Pour into a tall glass, add ice and top with grapefruit soda. Stir to combine.

TINGLY CUKES

SERVES 4

These shots will make your taste buds literally tingle. The secret is Szechuan peppercorns, which make your mouth feel all sorts of fun (if you've ever had mapo tofu, you know what it's like). This is a really fun drink to taste and discover with friends. Let the tingles take over and enjoy!

Super-Steeped Chamomile Tea

4 bags chamomile tea

½ cup hot water

Cocktail

1 cup seeded and chunked Persian or English cucumber

½ cup super-steeped chamomile tea (above), cooled

½ tbsp apple cider vinegar

5 dashes cucumber bitters or aromatic bitters

Zest and juice of 1 lemon

2 tbsp Szechuan peppercorns

2 tbsp granulated sugar

2 tsp coriander seeds

1 pinch salt

01 **Super-Steeped Chamomile Tea:** Place the tea bags in the hot water and let steep for 15 minutes. Remove the tea bags and let cool.

02 **Cocktail:** Place all ingredients in a blender and blend until smooth, 2 to 3 minutes. Strain through a fine-mesh strainer or nut milk bag into a clean container. Refrigerate for at least 1 hour before serving. Serve in chilled shot glasses.

OIL PAINTING

When seeking inspiration for recipes, I tend to look somewhere other than cocktails. In this case, I looked to art. One evening while strolling the stacks of Vancouver's central public library, I pulled out a book on oil paintings. The mood and vibe of still-life oil paintings is so vivid, you can almost smell the pungency of the scene. One of my favorite details in still-life kitchen paintings is the subtle, but often present, bouquet garni (a bundle of herbs used in cooking). And just like that, a new cocktail integrating deep citrus notes and a bouquet garni was born.

NOTE
Make sure to use really good-quality olive oil for this drink, since it's the star ingredient.

Quick Oleo Saccharum

1 cup loosely packed citrus peels (mix of lemon, lime and orange; adjust citrus ratio based on your preference)

1 cup granulated sugar

1 cup water

Cocktail

1 tbsp quick oleo saccharum (above), strained

4 tbsp non-alcoholic gin

2 tbsp freshly squeezed lemon juice

2 tbsp simple syrup

½ tsp good-quality extra virgin olive oil

Ice

Bouquet garni, to garnish (I use a bundle of thyme and a dried edible flower)

01 **Quick Oleo Saccharum:** Place the citrus peels and sugar in a pot and mash with a wooden spoon until the citrus is bruised. Add the water and bring to a low, gentle simmer over very low heat. Simmer for 10 minutes, making sure the water doesn't fully evaporate (if it does, add a splash more and remove from heat). Once off the heat, let cool completely. Place in a clean airtight container and store in the fridge for up to 1 week.

02 **Cocktail:** Place the oleo saccharum, non-alcoholic gin, lemon juice, simple syrup and olive oil in a shaker and dry shake for 1 minute. Add the ice and shake again until the shaker is frosty.

03 Strain into a coupe or similar glass. Garnish with the bouquet garni and serve.

ACKNOWLEDGMENTS

A big special thank-you to all my friends who helped me create this book. To Carl, Bri, Sophie, Brad and Dragan for your continuous love, support and generosity. It truly takes a village!

Thank you to Lindsay and Robert for believing in the idea behind this book and for helping me make it a reality, and to Jen for your design.

And a huge thank-you to all the people who have followed along my creative journey throughout the years, both online and offline. Your encouragement has allowed me to do what I love and share it with the world. I am one lucky guy!

Cheers to making creative dreams come true!

INDEX

A

agave syrup
Aloe, Montreal?, 57
Celery Soda, 72
The Evergreen, 130
Flaming Mary, 80
Gochu Soda, 141
Rhubarbara, 127
Sage Away, 124
almond
Go Bananas, 122
Halvachata, 39
Hazy Sunset, 27
Pineapple Jasmine
Cup, 109
Pomegranate Sour,
99
aloe vera juice
Aloe, Montreal?, 57
Floral Cozies, 35
Smooth Watermelon,
96
Apasionado, 91
aperitivo-style mixes, 12
Gochu Soda, 141
I'm Not Your Baby,
29
apple. See also cider
Apple of My Eye, 34
Granny's Fave, 95
Jazu!, 58
apricot: Hazy Sunset, 27

B

banana: Go Bananas,
122
beer (non-alcoholic)
Chavela, 66
Umamilada, 135
bitters, 11
Bitter Soda Float, 33
blackberry: I'm Not Your
Baby, 29
black currant: Purple
Clouds, 131

brine (olive/pickle)
The Dirrrty One, 62
Pickled Cooler, 136
Umamilada, 135

C

Calpico: Purple Clouds,
131
candy: Rita Rocks, 61
cantaloupe: A Shot of
Joy, 110
cardamom
Karat Gold, 98
Mango Tango, 105
Pineapple Jasmine
Cup, 109
Sage Away, 124
carrot: Karat Gold, 98
celery
Celery Soda, 72
Chavela, 66
Flaming Mary, 80
Rita Rocks, 61
Thai Basil Fizz Soda,
66–67
Chavela, 66
cherry
Pomegranate Sour,
99
Sleepy Cherries, 40
chlorophyll: The
Evergreen, 130
chocolate: Cocoamoco
Seltzer, 75
cider (non-alcoholic)
Apple of My Eye, 34
Golden Hour, 54
La Flor, 102
Plum Blossom Shrub,
121
cinnamon
Halvachata, 39
Oh My Glögg, 86
Pear Cinnamon
Hearts, 98

Pomegranate Sour,
99
Sesame Blanket, 45
Sleepy Cherries, 40
Tepache Punch, 128
Walnut Chai Dos
Leches, 78
citrus. See also specific
citrus flavors
Oil Painting, 144
cloves
La Flor, 102
Oh My Glögg, 86
Tepache Punch, 128
Walnut Chai Dos
Leches, 78
Cocoamoco Seltzer, 75
coconut
Cojicha, 34
The Glow, 112
Green Coconuts, 77
Karat Gold, 98
Smooth Watermelon,
96
Umbrella Bella, 42
coffee
Cocoamoco Seltzer,
75
Cojicha, 34
Nuttyrato, 138
cranberry: Crandelion,
47
cucumber
The Dirrrty One, 62
Mango Tango, 105
Pickled Cooler, 136
Shiso Cuke Sour, 64
Thai Basil Fizz Soda,
66–67
Tingly Cukes, 143

D

The Dirrrty One, 62

E

Echinacea Trance, 24
elderflower: Fountain of
Beauty, 92
The Evergreen, 130

F

fennel (seed): Sesame
Blanket, 45
Fire and Grass, 30
Flaming Mary, 80
Floral Cozies, 35
flowers. See also
hibiscus; lavender
Crandelion, 47
Fountain of Beauty,
92
La Flor, 102
foamer (cocktail), 11
Crandelion, 47
Pear Cinnamon
Hearts, 98
Pineapple Jasmine
Cup, 109
Pomegranate Sour,
99
Shiso Cuke Sour, 64
Fountain of Beauty, 92

G

gin (non-alcoholic)
Apasionado, 91
The Dirrrty One, 62
Echinacea Trance, 24
Lychee Loca, 106
Oil Painting, 144
Pickled Cooler, 136
Umbrella Bella, 42
ginger
Ginger Glam, 88
A Shot of Joy, 110
The Glow, 112
Go Bananas, 122
gochujang: Gochu
Soda, 141

Golden Hour, 54
Granny's Fave, 95
grape
    The Dirrrty One, 62
    Fountain of Beauty,
        92
    Grape Stallion, 118
grapefruit
    Bitter Soda Float, 33
    Floral Cozies, 35
    Gochu Soda, 141
    Grape Stallion, 118
    Margaloma Float, 67
Green Coconuts, 77
grenadine: Golden
        Hour, 54
Guava Brava, 70

H
Halvachata, 39
hazelnut: Nuttyrato, 138
Hazy Sunset, 27
herbs. See also mint
    La Flor, 102
    Oil Painting, 144
    Sage Away, 124
    Thai Basil Fizz Soda,
        66
hibiscus
    Bitter Dusk, 48
    La Flor, 102
hojicha. See tea, green

I
ice, 11
I'm Not Your Baby, 29

J
jicama: Jazu!, 58
juniper berries
    Grape Stallion, 118
    La Flor, 102
    Mango Tango, 105
    Sage Away, 124

K
Karat Gold, 98
kombucha: Woody
        Booch, 131

L
La Flor, 102

lavender
    Floral Cozies, 35
    Purple Clouds, 131
lemon
    Apasionado, 91
    Bitter Dusk, 48
    Flaming Mary, 80
    The Glow, 112
    Granny's Fave, 95
    La Flor, 102
    Mango Tango, 105
    Rita Rocks, 61
    Sage Away, 124
    A Shot of Joy, 110
    Tingly Cukes, 143
lemongrass: Fire and
        Grass, 30
lime
    Aloe, Montreal?, 57
    Chavela, 66
    The Evergreen, 130
    Lychee Loca, 106
    Mango Tango, 105
    Margaloma Float, 67
    Oh My Glögg, 86
    Pineapple Jasmine
        Cup, 109
    Rita Rocks, 61
    Smooth Watermelon,
        96
    Thai Basil Fizz Soda,
        66
    Umamilada, 135
Lychee Loca, 106

M
Mango Tango, 105
maple syrup
    Apple of My Eye, 34
    Cocoamoco Seltzer,
        75
Margaloma Float, 67
milk and creamer (dairy/
        non-dairy)
    Cocoamoco Seltzer,
        75
    Cojicha, 34
    Halvachata, 39
    Walnut Chai Dos
        Leches, 78
mint
    Aloe, Montreal?, 57

The Evergreen, 130
Lychee Loca, 106
miso: Flaming Mary, 80
mood drinks, 4
    ingredients, 11
    tools and glassware, 7
mushroom: Umamilada,
        135

N
nutmeg
    Halvachata, 39
    Sleepy Cherries, 40
Nuttyrato, 138

O
Oh My Glögg, 86
olive. See also brine
    Flaming Mary, 80
olive oil: Oil Painting,
        144
orange
    Apasionado, 91
    Bitter Dusk, 48
    Crandelion, 47
    The Glow, 112
    Go Bananas, 122
    Golden Hour, 54
    La Flor, 102
    Oh My Glögg, 86
    Rhubarbara, 127
    Sleepy Cherries, 40
    Tepache Punch, 128
    Woody Booch, 131
orange blossom water
    The Glow, 112
    A Shot of Joy, 110
orgeat syrup. See
        almond

P
passion fruit:
        Apasionado, 91
Pear Cinnamon Hearts,
        98
pepper (spice)
    Golden Hour, 54
    Jazu!, 58
    Sage Away, 124
    Tepache Punch, 128
    Thai Basil Fizz Soda,
        66

Tingly Cukes, 143
peppers (hot)
    Flaming Mary, 80
    Gochu Soda, 141
    Granny's Fave, 95
Pickled Cooler, 136
pineapple
    La Flor, 102
    Lychee Loca, 106
    Pineapple Jasmine
        Cup, 109
    Tepache Punch, 128
plum
    Plum Blossom Shrub,
        121
    A Shot of Joy, 110
pomegranate. See also
        grenadine
    Oh My Glögg, 86
    Pomegranate Sour,
        99
Pop Rocks: Rita Rocks,
        61
Purple Clouds, 131

R
Rhubarbara, 127
Rita Rocks, 61
rose water: Smoking
        Guns n' Roses, 22

S
Sage Away, 124
salt, 11
seltzer/club soda
    Celery Soda, 72
    Cocoamoco Seltzer,
        75
    Pickled Cooler, 136
    Tepache Punch, 128
Sesame Blanket, 45
Shiso Cuke Sour, 64
A Shot of Joy, 110
Sleepy Cherries, 40
smoke, 11
    Fire and Grass, 30
    Smoking Guns n'
        Roses, 22
    Woody Booch, 131
Smooth Watermelon, 96
sorbet
    Bitter Soda Float, 33

Margaloma Float, 67
Rita Rocks, 61
soy sauce: Umamilada, 135
spices, 11. *See also specific spices*
Aloe, Montreal?, 57
Fountain of Beauty, 92
Guava Brava, 70
Margaloma Float, 67
Pickled Cooler, 136
Tingly Cukes, 143
spirits (non-alcoholic), 12. *See also* gin
strawberry: Rhubarbara, 127
syrups, 12. *See also specific syrups*

T
tea, black
Apple of My Eye, 34
Ginger Glam, 88
Go Bananas, 122
Grape Stallion, 118
Walnut Chai Dos Leches, 78
tea, chamomile
Floral Cozies, 35
Mango Tango, 105
Pear Cinnamon Hearts, 98

Rhubarbara, 127
Tingly Cukes, 143
tea, green
Celery Soda, 72
Cojicha, 34
Granny's Fave, 95
Green Coconuts, 77
Margaloma Float, 67
Nuttyrato, 138
Rita Rocks, 61
Sage Away, 124
tea, herbal, 12. *See also* tea, chamomile
Bitter Dusk, 48
Crandelion, 47
Echinacea Trance, 24
Fire and Grass, 30
Plum Blossom Shrub, 121
tea, jasmine
Mango Tango, 105
Pineapple Jasmine Cup, 109
A Shot of Joy, 110
Tepache Punch, 128
Thai Basil Fizz Soda, 66
Tingly Cukes, 143
tomato
Chavela, 66
Flaming Mary, 80
Umamilada, 135
tonic water
Bitter Dusk, 48

Karat Gold, 98
Rhubarbara, 127
Smoking Guns n' Roses, 22
turmeric
The Glow, 112
Golden Hour, 54

U
Umamilada, 135
Umbrella Bella, 42
umeboshi: A Shot of Joy, 110

V
vanilla
Apasionado, 91
Bitter Soda Float, 33
Cocoamoco Seltzer, 75
Cojicha, 34
Floral Cozies, 35
Granny's Fave, 95
Halvachata, 39
La Flor, 102
Nuttyrato, 138
Oh My Glögg, 86
Pear Cinnamon Hearts, 98
Pomegranate Sour, 99
Purple Clouds, 131
Rhubarbara, 127

Tepache Punch, 128
vinegar and verjus
Apple of My Eye, 34
Flaming Mary, 80
Fountain of Beauty, 92
Grape Stallion, 118
Guava Brava, 70
Plum Blossom Shrub, 121
Tingly Cukes, 143

W
Walnut Chai Dos Leches, 78
Watermelon, Smooth, 96
wine (non-alcoholic)
Fountain of Beauty, 92
The Glow, 112
Oh My Glögg, 86
Woody Booch, 131
Worcestershire: Chavela, 66

Y
yuzu
Jazu!, 58
Karat Gold, 98